# THE DEVELOPMENT
# OF THE
# MODERN STATE

# MAIN THEMES IN EUROPEAN HISTORY

*Bruce Mazlish, General Editor*

# THE DEVELOPMENT
# OF THE
# MODERN STATE

Heinz Lubasz
*Brandeis University*

THE MACMILLAN COMPANY

COLLIER-MACMILLAN LIMITED, LONDON

The Macmillan Company
866 Third Avenue, New York, New York 10022
COLLIER-MACMILLAN CANADA, LTD., TORONTO, ONTARIO

Printed in the United States of America

# FOREWORD

History, we are frequently told, is a seamless web. However, by isolating and studying the strands that compose the tapestry of man's past, we are able to discern the pattern, or patterns, of which it is comprised. Such an effort does not preclude a grasp of the warp and woof, and the interplay of the strands; rather, it eventually demands and facilitates such a comprehension. It is with this in mind that the individual volumes of the MAIN THEMES series have been conceived.

The student will discover, for example, that the population changes discussed in one volume relate to the changes in technology traced in another volume; that both changes are affected by, and affect in turn, religious and intellectual developments; and that all of these changes and many more ramify into a complicated historical network through all the volumes. In following through this complex interrelationship of the parts, the student recreates for himself the unity of history.

Each volume achieves its purpose, and its appeal to a general audience, by presenting the best articles by experts in the field of history and allied disciplines. In a number of cases, the articles have been translated into English for the first time. The individual volume editor has linked these contributions into an integrated account of his theme, and supplied a selected bibliography by means of footnotes for the student who wishes to pursue the subject further. The introduction is an original treatment of the problems in the particular field. It provides continuity and background for the articles, points out gaps in the existing literature, offers new interpretations, and suggests further research.

The volumes in this series afford the student of history an unusual opportunity to explore subjects either not treated, or touched upon lightly in a survey text. Some examples are population—the dramatis personae of history; war—the way of waging peace by other means; the rise of technology and science in relation to society; the role of religious and cultural ideas and institutions; the continuous ebb and flow of exploration and colonialism; and the political and economic works contrived by modern man. Holding fast to these Ariadne threads, the student penetrates the fascinating labyrinth of history.

BRUCE MAZLISH
*General Editor*

# CONTENTS

# INTRODUCTION

"An nescis, mi fili, quantilla prudentia regitur orbis?"
—Count Oxenstierna (1583–1654)
(Knowest thou not, my son, with how little wisdom the
world is governed?)

The first thing to be said about *the* modern state is that it does not exist and never has existed. What has existed historically is a great number of modern states, with very varied constitutions, internal political lives, and international careers. When, therefore, we speak of *the* modern state, we speak of an abstraction concocted of common denominators, of features common to many or most such states much of the time, but certainly not to be met with in precisely the same forms in *all* such states, nor in any one of them over a very long period of time. When I speak, in what follows, of "the modern state," I shall, therefore, be speaking of what social scientists nowadays generally call a "model" or—more nearly, perhaps—of what Max Weber called an "ideal type." In dealing with the modern state in this very general and more or less abstract fashion—the articles that follow deal with concrete details of its historical development—we may hope to achieve a measure of systematic clarity as to some of its essential characteristics. But our ideal type will be ideal in the sense that it will not, without substantial modifications, qualifications, and exceptions, correctly or adequately describe any *one* of the many structures properly called "modern states."

## I

The modern state is a European, or more exactly, western European, creation. It gradually emerged in the course of the fifteenth and sixteenth centuries and found its first mature form in the seventeenth. It is worth noting that the modern state came into existence in the same area and during the same period as did modern capitalism, modern science and philosophy, and that specifically modern form of Christianity, Protestantism. The simultaneous emergence of distinctively new forms of political, economic, intellectual, and religious life is by no means a matter of mere coincidence. All forms of human activity are, as we know, to some degree interconnected, though the extent to which they display common features will, of course, vary a great deal. Suffice it to say that a remarkable change in the style and focus of human activity is discernible in western Europe in the era of the Renaissance, which leaves its mark on almost every aspect of civilization. Men's activities appear to become more systematic, intensive, and secular. Modern capitalism is more relentless in its pursuit of gain, and more proficient and advanced in its techniques, than medieval capitalism; modern science is less restrained in its quest for knowledge of *all* kinds, and more concerned with method, than medieval; and Protestantism, by drawing a sharper line between the sacred and the secular, between God and man, than medieval Christianity had done, allows men to pursue their worldly goals with almost undivided attention, even if it enjoins them to do so for the greater glory of God.

This increased attention to technical proficiency (skill, method, efficiency, specialization, routine, the appropriateness of means to ends), coupled with a heightened goal-directed dynamism (single-minded, intensive, and very nearly limitless pursuit of an objective) and with a significant separation of this-worldly from other-worldly considerations, is also very much in evidence in political life. The state (which at first means the ruler, the prince) comes to employ ever more efficient means to pursue, with great intensity and to the full extent of available resources, one principal objective: the accumulation of power (cf. Ritter). From its inception, the modern state seeks to acquire sole authority and effective power within a given territory, as well as autonomy vis-à-vis other states. Exclusive domination over a certain territory and its population (the ruler's domain, the dynasty's realm, the king's inheritance) and the power to be the arbiter of its own conduct in relations among states—that is the twin aspect of modern sovereignty, the Janus face of the modern state. The modern state is, first of all, the sovereign state.

Exclusive domination does not in itself mean unlimited or total domination. The modern state is, in fact, not only a sovereign state; it is also a state governed by a public and more or less stable system of law, which regulates an ever-growing number of activities and of relationships among individuals and groups in society, but also regulates the state itself and sets some sort of limit to the operations of government. The modern state claims exclusive and compulsory jurisdiction over its subjects or citizens, but it exercises this claim in accordance with set and known procedures, and, normally at least, it does not punish acts that have not previously been declared to be punishable. Furthermore, the modern state claims only to *regulate* or *control* economic, social, or even religious and cultural activities: it does not itself *undertake* these activities or attempt to absorb them into the state. There is a distinction between state and society, between the formal, public "organization of the community for the purposes of government" (Kitson Clark), and society itself—the sum-total of citizens and their nongovernmental organizations and activities; a distinction, in short, between what is public and concerns the state and what is private and none of its business. The maintenance of this distinction, no matter how imperfectly, is absolutely fundamental to the modern state. It is the very foundation not only of the rights of the citizen or subject, but also of at least a measure of free economic, social, and cultural activity of whatever kind. The drawing of a distinction between state and society is, in short, itself a fundamental characteristic of the modern state.

In a similar way, the state's claim to be the sole arbiter of its own actions vis-à-vis other states does not necessarily mean that it claims to destroy all other states and to establish dominion over the whole globe. On the contrary, the modern state is, in fact, not only a sovereign state; it is also a state that recognizes, even if it does not always respect, the sovereignty of other states. Hence from the sixteenth century to the twentieth, Europe has more or less adhered to the principle of a balance of power and has developed an international law, not to prevent war, but to regulate the conduct of states in war as well as in peace. That the principle of balance of power frequently led to war is not an argument against it, since it was not intended, any more than international law was, to preserve the peace, but only to serve as a regulative principle that would allow many sovereign states to exist side by side. There is a difference between claiming sovereign autonomy and claiming world domination; between regarding another political entity as an adversary to be worsted or defeated, and regarding it as an enemy to be utterly vanquished or even destroyed. The recognition of this difference is absolutely fundamental to the modern state system, and hence to the existence of the modern state as a power-unit. It is the very foundation not only of limited war, but also of a regulated and orderly peace. The reciprocal recognition of sovereignty is, in short, likewise a fundamental characteristic of the modern state.

## II

The first modern states arose in Italy, England, France, and Spain. The Italian principality, partly because of its small size, did not as such serve as a model for later developments (cf. Ritter), though it was the first to evolve a number of institutions—notably the bureaucratic administration and the mercenary army (cf. Chabod)—typical of the state throughout the modern era. Spain, which did exert considerable influence on the emerging patterns of the modern state in the sixteenth and seventeenth, and to some degree even in the eighteenth, centuries, both in Europe and overseas (cf. Chabod, Lefebvre), subsequently went into decline, and its influence on the evolution of the modern state was thereafter very slight. England and France, however, which had been the strongest of medieval monarchies (a fact thoroughly relevant to their becoming the most powerful and influential of modern states) became, each in its way, models for other states. For the development of *European* states the example of France was paramount; as a continental state itself, its geopolitical situation and its economic and social conditions were in many ways similar to those of other continental states, and its political institutions were, as a result, widely imitated, both before the French Revolution (absolute monarchy) and after (constitutionalism). England, whose development during the Middle Ages and until the nineteenth century was in some important respects different from that of the continent, had a greater impact on the *non-European* world (largely via its colonies, especially the American colonies) than on Europe itself, though in the nineteenth century, if not indeed earlier, some of its institutions, too, were adapted to continental practice. At the risk of considerable oversimplification we may say that England is the prototype of the parliamentary, constitutional state, in which local self-government provides for a substantial degree of decentralization; while France is the prototype of the authoritarian (which does not, of course, necessarily mean dictatorial) regime with a highly centralized, bureaucratic administration (cf. Hintze).

In France, and in most of the states of continental Europe, including the many small principalities, dukedoms, and kingdoms in Germany and Italy, a permanent bureaucracy and a standing army were the principal technical tools with which the modern state was built, and it was money that enabled the ruler to acquire them. The availability of fluid wealth made it possible for him to replace the feudal nobility, in the two functions that in the Middle Ages had made it indispensable to him, with hired professionals. With the rise of a professional bureaucracy and a professional army, the nobility also lost the important political role it had once held in the state. As it now had little actual power, either military or administrative, and as, by the terms of its own cherished privileges, it was largely exempt from substantial taxation (it simply collected the peasants' taxes) and therefore did not directly supply much of the state's income, the king could afford to ignore it politically. The great councils and the assemblies of estates, which had played so important a role in the medieval "monarchy of estates," were in the absolute monarchies of the seventeenth century gradually "put to sleep" (Lousse). For two centuries or more (i.e., until the era of the middle-class revolutions), the monarchs of continental Europe, including those of Prussia and Russia, even managed to obtain the active or passive support of this nobility, by allowing it extensive social and economic privileges, and a very nearly free hand with the peasantry (cf. Lefebvre).

But the very element that had made it possible for the prince to build his state—to wit, money—also proved to be the source of his undoing. As the state expanded its activities, as it enlarged its army and its administration, and as funds were lavished on the pomp and luxury with which the absolute monarch liked to surround himself, the state's need for ready cash constantly grew. The principal producers of cash were the commercial and industrial middle class and the peasantry. Though both these classes felt the heavy hand of the tax collector and the oppressive weight of state-imposed restrictions and regulations of many kinds, and though both bitterly resented the privileges and the wealth of a largely unproductive, parasitical aristocracy, the bourgeoisie alone was able, in the late eighteenth and in the nineteenth century, to carry through revolutions which sharply curtailed or even abolished both the privileged status of the aristocracy and the authority of the monarch. Thus the bourgeoisie acquired a measure of control over the state which it had been so largely financing.

These revolutions radically transformed the conception of the state in respect of its physical and human foundations. The bourgeois revolutions were carried through in the name (though not to the benefit) of *all* the state's population, of the whole *nation,* in the name of natural rights and popular sovereignty. Thus the state, which had hitherto been thought of as the domain and personal inheritance of the king, as the king's land, was henceforward conceived to "belong" instead to the people who inhabited it, to the nation. It is with the era of the bourgeois revolutions that the state ceases to be, in fact as well as in conception, a *proprietary-territorial state* and becomes

instead a *nation-state*. And just as it was France that had served as
the principal model of the absolutistic, dynastic state, so it was chiefly
France that inspired, by example and by reaction against it, the building
elsewhere in Europe of the liberalistic nation-state.

In England, as we have noted, the whole course of development
was somewhat different. During the Middle Ages, feudalism and
monarchy had evolved in England along lines that differed more
or less markedly from continental patterns; and it is to a great extent
because of these peculiarities that, in the modern period also, the
English monarchy—one hardly dare speak of "the English *state*" [1]—
has followed a path that diverges from the European norm. It will
suffice for our present purpose to say that in England the feudal lord
was less wealthy and less powerful (relative both to the king and to
the rest of the population) than his continental counterpart; and that
the rest of the rural population was less poor and less abject in its
condition than most of the continental peasantry. What is more, there
existed a substantial range of landholders of middling rank and prosperity, who were neither feudal lords nor landless agricultural laborers,
and whose wealthier members fused with the lesser aristocracy into the
so-called "gentry" of the sixteenth and seventeenth centuries. The very
existence and the strength of this intermediate class proved a serious
and effective obstacle to the growth of royal bureaucracy and royal
militarism in England. Furthermore, this gentry, being neither so
proud as the continental aristocracy nor so humble as the continental
peasantry, did not find it difficult, when occasion arose, to make common cause with the middle classes of the towns.

Occasion did arise. When, in the early seventeenth century, the
Stuart dynasty, following the common pattern of European absolutism,
tried to put Parliament to sleep, to govern through the king's henchmen and to keep a standing army in peacetime, a large part of the
gentry and of the urban middle class joined the rebellion against the
king, which ended with the king literally losing his head, after which
England was for some few years a republic. When the monarchy was
restored—though another, very tame, revolution was required to make
matters quite clear and definite—provision was made for ensuring
the continued active existence of Parliament, securing "the rights of
Englishmen," and making the king dependent upon Parliament for
the money with which to finance both the administration and the
military. In addition, the gentry, together with some of the aristocracy
and some of bourgeoisie, formed a "governing class" which, through
its role in national as well as in local government, in fact constituted

the backbone of the English polity. The English revolutions of the seventeenth century (1642, 1688) gave expression to libertarian and republican ideas which in the following century were to inspire both England's own American colonists and the middle classes of several European states, notably France, to overthrow the despots (enlightened or otherwise) [2] who ruled them, and to adopt one form or another of constitutional government (cf. Hintze).

In the nineteenth century the distinctive achievements of the English monarchy (parliamentary government—by a small oligarchy; constitutionalism without a written constitution; a tradition of liberty; and a considerable measure of local self-government—by the same small oligarchy) are fused with the distinctive achievements of the French state (centralized government; bureaucratic administration; formal, written constitutions; a tradition of militarism) to form the more or less liberal, bourgeois nation-state (cf. Harris). The monarch's power is either substantially reduced or altogether abolished, and the chief power in the state is now economic power, the power of the truly wealthy among the commercial and industrial middle class. The old aristocracy continues to play a role in the state, thanks to its positions in bureaucracy and army. Its political role actually increases, but now depends on wealth rather than privilege. The power of property either is formally expressed through the restriction of the suffrage (as, for example, in England and France) or makes itself felt unofficially where property restrictions on the right to vote are slight (as in the United States). The politically dominant position of wealth is given justification by the appeal to the natural right of property (much as the dominant position of the monarch in the seventeenth and eighteenth centuries had been justified by the appeal to the divine right of kingship): those who have the greatest material stake in the state are entitled directly or indirectly to control it.

At the same time the population as a whole, under the impact of the powerful ideology of nationalism, is called upon loyally to serve the interests of the bourgeois nation-state (much as religious ideology had formerly been effective in keeping the people loyal and obedient to the monarch). In particular (and this constitutes a change from previous practice whose importance can hardly be exaggerated), the mass of the population is henceforward either induced or coerced into swelling the state's military forces in time of war. When, with the total wars of the twentieth century, the whole population becomes not only liable to military service but also the wholesale object of military assault, the territorial state ceases to be an impenetrable power-unit (cf. Herz). At the same time and by the same token, the distinction between soldier and civilian virtually disappears. With the emergence of total war (whose roots lie in the nation-at-arms of the French Revolution), it is no longer the armed might of the *state* but all the resources of *society*—from economy to "civilian" population—that is pitted against the enemy and becomes the object of destruction. It is with World War I that we can first clearly detect the *breakdown of the distinction between state and society* which signalizes the beginning of the end of the modern state (cf. Rothfels). In this sense total war is intimately related to the totalitarian systems, Left and Right, which deliberately set about the destruction of the modern state.

## III

Throughout the nineteenth century, the painful involvement of the mass of the population with the destinies of the state in time of war, coupled with the profound and, for the lower classes, generally deleterious effects of the industrial revolution, powerfully stimulated the demand of the lower middle class and the working class for a voice in the affairs of the state. This took the form of a demand for the vote or, alternatively, for further revolution. In the later nineteenth century and in the twentieth, the exclusion of the less wealthy and the propertyless from a share in government led to a more or less militant campaign for genuine political democracy. This campaign was at length successful in many European states, with the introduction of universal suffrage—strikingly enough, after the extraordinary exertions and sacrifices demanded of populations in World War I.

At the same time (i.e., in the nineteenth century and after) a powerful movement grew up which sought to counteract the gross economic and social injustices and the manifest ills which resulted from the rapid development of industrial capitalism, the equally rapid spread of congested, unsanitary, and oppressive living and working conditions, and the inequitable distribution of the wealth which industrial capital and labor jointly produced (cf. Kitson Clark). Socialist and labor movements aimed to combat these conditions either through the establishment of political democracy, which should give the worker some *indirect* control over industry by allowing him a voice in the councils of state; or through social and economic measures, not excluding revolution, which should give him *direct* control over industry to a greater or less degree. In the extreme case, the problems of the worker were to be solved by making all industry, business, and agriculture the property of society as a whole, rather than of individual entrepreneurs, and by overthrowing the bourgeois nation-state altogether.

Where the movement for political democracy has been successful, the modern state has in essentials survived, though its political operations have been to some extent altered, not least by the rise of a class of professional politicians. (In mass democracy, political parties have themselves to be systematically organized—cf. Chabod—and the first qualification for political office becomes the ability to get elected.) Where, on the other hand, the movement for social equality has been successful, it has taken one of two forms: the limited social democracy of the Welfare State, which is indeed a form of the modern state; or the unlimited social totalitarianism of the Communist system, within which the modern state is largely destroyed. To be more precise, Communism abolishes the distinction between state and society which, as we indicated above, is itself crucial to the existence of the modern state, as being the essential precondition of a public and more or less stable legal order, and as setting a limit to *the extent to which society is organized for the purposes of government.*

State control over the economy is, of course, quite compatible with the existence of the modern state; indeed, the modern state has, historically, always exercised some control over the economy, though the extent of that control has varied a great deal. Workers' control of the particular enterprises in which they are engaged is, to judge by certain Scandinavian examples, likewise compatible with the existence of the modern state. But *totalitarian socialism* [3] (i.e., Communism, as distinct from democratic socialism), which goes beyond *control* of the entrepreneur to itself *becoming* the entrepreneur, undermines the distinction between state and society, between what is absorbed into governmental organization and what is left alone. In order to mobilize and control all the resources of society, Communism organizes and regiments not only economic activity, but almost every form of social, cultural, and intellectual life as well. Family life, leisure time, thought, science, and the arts—in short, everything that in the typical modern state belongs to the realm of private life *not* organized for the purposes of government—all this becomes so thoroughly subject to governmental organization that it is scarcely possible any longer to distinguish the state from society. Whether one calls this the destruction of society by the state, or the destruction of the state by society, is largely a matter of taste and terminology.

This *total* organization of society into a totalitarian socialist system is given justification in terms of the historical right of labor, much as absolutism uses the divine right of kingship and bourgeois liberalism uses the natural right of property as a justification for the political system. The totalitarian form of socialism takes over the bureaucratic techniques and the monopoly of military power developed by the modern state; but it largely destroys the stable legal order in terms of which the modern state has functioned. It substitutes what is called "socialist legality," which replaces the legal order of the modern state with a process in which laws, orders, procedures, and the actual measures taken, are all derived, supposedly from the "objective" needs of society, but in fact from the more or less arbitrary will of the ruler. As a result, Communism is more arbitrary and more tyrannical, and controls human activity to an infinitely greater degree, than the most absolute of monarchs had done in the early centuries of the modern state.

If totalitarian socialism is the total organization of society in the supposed interest of labor, *totalitarian capitalism* [3] (i.e., Fascism, as distinct from democratic capitalism) is the total organization of society in the supposed interest of capital, which is somehow made to seem identical with the national interest. Fascism thus perpetuates and tightens the link between bourgeois capitalism and the ideology of nationalism which was forged in the nineteenth century. In what it claims are the interests at once of the nation as a whole and of big business in particular, totalitarian capitalism, instead of taking over both the *human* and the *physical* means of production (factories, businesses, land) as Communism does, takes over only the *human* means of production—the workers. Fascism destroys not only the democratic political institutions, but also the economic institutions (unions, labor law, collective bargaining) by means of which the workers have improved their situation. It ruthlessly regiments the working population, and solves the problem of unemployment by means of public works, arms production, and large-scale military service. At the same time it allows big capital (and even small) a more or less free hand, provides it with cheap labor (by controlling wages), and affords it enormous financial gain by the fantastic increase in the production of armaments which—needless to say—is said to be essential to the national interest. As Communism does, but for a completely different main purpose, Fascism subjects the whole range of social existence to organization for the purposes of government; the distinction between state and society is abolished; and the stable legal order of the modern state is replaced by the arbitrary will of the leader.

But whereas socialist totalitarianism mobilizes and organizes society for the primary purpose of creating a new sort of society, capitalist totalitarianism mobilizes and organizes society for the primary purpose

of waging war. Whereas Communism promises to bring in the millennium the world over, by securing the historical right of labor,
Fascism promises to bring in the millennium for its own nation only,
by securing the natural right of the superior nation. Consequently,
whereas socialist totalitarianism typically makes war by economic and
political means, including revolution, on a world-wide class (the
bourgeoisie), capitalist totalitarianism typically makes war by military
means on other nations or, in the extreme case, on the whole rest of
the globe. Communism, in other words, aims to replace the world
of sovereign nation-states with a single classless society; Fascism aims to
replace the world of sovereign nation-states with the world-wide
supremacy of a single nation. Thus totalitarianism, whether of the Left
or of the Right, and making due allowance for differences between
them, not only destroys the modern state *internally*, as a form of political organization; it also threatens to destroy the modern state *externally*,
as the member of a system of sovereign states.

## IV

The modern sovereign state, which came into existence in the
ferment of the Renaissance, is in danger of succumbing amidst the
multiple crises of the twentieth century.

In that part of the world in which it has been the predominant
form of governmental organization for more than four centuries it
survives, at least for the time being, in modified form. It is being modified internally, through the Welfare State, in the direction of greater
governmental control over society, i.e., of intensified sovereignty;
externally it is being modified, through international organization and
cooperation, in the direction of a lessened independence in international
affairs, i.e., of reduced sovereignty.

In the non-European world, new states are coming into existence
in conditions which differ profoundly from those in which the modern
state first arose. The new states of Africa and Asia are being born into
a world in which, given the vulnerability of all states to nuclear attack
(cf. Herz), *full* autonomy vis-à-vis other states is unattainable to them
from the start; and in which *limited* control over society may seem to be
inadequate to deal with the enormous tasks of economic, social, and
cultural development which is mandatory in all the areas of the world
which are seriously underdeveloped.

Totalitarianism is born of crisis, of the felt need to mobilize all the
resources of society to meet some extraordinary challenge, to tackle some
extraordinary task. Whether the highly developed countries of Europe

and North America can avoid the critical breakdowns which invite totalitarian expedients; and whether the underdeveloped countries of Asia, Africa, and Latin America can meet the critical challenge of rapid development without recourse to totalitarian solutions—these are, on the domestic, on the social side, the crucial issues which will determine whether the modern state will be succeeded by another limited, or by an unlimited, form of organizing society for purposes of government.

But there is another area of crisis besides the domestic one. The crisis of total war, and of the constant and imminent threat of total war, makes for totalitarian solutions just as surely as does social crisis. And it is only reasonable to say that, unless this crisis too can be averted or resolved by peaceful means, it is almost certain that it will be the unlimited domination of totalitarian systems which will succeed the limited domination of the modern state.

## BIBLIOGRAPHY

Dowdall, H. C., The Word "State," London, 1923.

Hintze, Otto, "Wesen und Wandlung des modernen Staats," in Hintze, Staat und Verfassung, 2nd ed., Göttingen, 1962, pp. 470–496.

Kjellén, R., Der Staat als Lebensform, 4th ed., Berlin-Grunewald, 1924 (tr. from Swedish).

Krabbe, H., The Modern Idea of the State, New York and London, 1927 (tr. from German).

Laski, H. J., The State in Theory and Practice, New York, 1935.

Lindsay, A. D., The Modern Democratic State, London, 1943 (repr. New York, 1962).

MacIver, R. M., The Modern State, London, 1926.

Meinecke, F., Machiavellism, New Haven, Conn., 1957 (tr. from German).

Meyer, A. O., "Zur Geschichte des Wortes Staat," in Welt als Geschichte, 10 (1950), pp. 229–239.

Michel, H., L'idée de l'état, Paris, 1896.

Näf, W., Staat und Staatsgedanke, Bern, 1935, esp. "Der geschichtliche Aufbau des modernen Staates," pp. 29–46.

Oppenheimer, F., The state; its history and development viewed sociologically, Indianapolis, Ind., 1914 (tr. from German).

Weber, Max, Staatssoziologie (ed. J. Winckelmann), Berlin, 1956.

## NOTES

[1] In English constitutional law and theory, "state" has never become a technically precise term, though in recent years it has perhaps come to be more frequently used than formerly. Even in ordinary usage, however, "government" and "kingdom" are terms used to describe what in other countries would be called the state.

[2] It should be noted that though the American colonists fancied them-

selves oppressed by that "tyrant," George III, it was Parliament, if anyone, that was doing the oppressing.

[3] Neither Communism nor Fascism is a purely economic phenomenon, though in both systems the totalitarian organization of the economy is a vital element. For additional perspectives on totalitarianism, see the article by Mr. Kennan, below, and the works listed in the bibliography appended to it.

# ORIGINS OF THE MODERN STATE [*]

## Gerhard Ritter

*The historical roots of the modern state must be sought, as Professor Ritter (Professor emeritus of Modern History, University of Freiburg, Germany) shows, as far back as the High Middle Ages. As it emerges out of the anarchy of the decaying feudal system, the embryonic modern state already displays the relentless quest for power that remains one of its hallmarks throughout its history.*

## I. *Disintegration of the* Res Publica Christiana *and Formation of a European State System*

It used to be thought that a single event, if possible even a specific date, could be taken as separating "Middle Ages" from "Modern Times." Thus it was long customary to regard Columbus' discovery of America (1492) or the French invasion of Italy (1494) as the watershed between the two epochs. By now we know perfectly well that the crucial change in man's sensibility which occurred in the sixteenth century had little if anything to do with the expansion of geographical horizons or the invention of new devices. Unquestionably a new era opened when history moved from a European to a world-wide stage. But the full effect of this change on political practice and on the minds of men made itself felt only in the course of many generations. Even the sudden emergence of a new "state system" spanning all of Europe, which seems to be observable in the foreign invasions of Italy from 1494 on, proves on closer inspection to be an illusion.

[*] Gerhard Ritter, *Die Neugestaltung Europas im 16. Jahrhundert*, Berlin: Verlag des Druckhauses Tempelhof, 1950, pp. 19–28. Translated by Heinz Lubasz with permission of Verlag Ullstein, Darmstadt.

This state system had at least partially developed and established itself in the course of several centuries. In the Italian wars it merely underwent a significant extension, all its energies being dramatically brought into play on a single spot.

It is not a single event that marks the transition from the medieval to the modern world, but a gradual transformation—a transformation of intellectual, social, economic and political life. The political face of Europe began to change early. The intellectual and the social unity of the West, however, endured in essentials until the close of the Middle Ages: the unity of the church, of learning, art and fable, of the matter and forms of poetry, of the intellectual world as a whole; as well as the sense of community that informed the several ranks of society—the clergy and the feudal nobility especially—which cut across national boundaries. But the political foundations of this unity had already crumbled in the thirteenth century.

The foundations were destroyed by the conflict of Empire and Papacy. When these two pinnacles of the *universitas Christiana* became locked in irreconcilable conflict, the whole edifice began to totter. When the German Empire was at last defeated, chaos set in both south and north of the Alps. The once vigorous Empire was replaced by a multitude of principalities and cities engaged in bloody feuds with one another. The political center of gravity shifted decisively from the middle of Europe to the west. The Empire, with its nebulous claims to universal authority, would henceforward be able to count for something only in the hands of a dynasty whose real strength lay in its possession of substantial power outside of Germany.

The future belonged to the national states of western Europe, where strong monarchs allied themselves with the great nations that were slowly awakening to self-consciousness. The political world of northern and eastern Europe was for a long time unable to attain a similar internal cohesiveness. But even there, under national dynasties, there now arose power structures of enormous extent which not only threw off every memory of former feudal dependence on the German emperor but, from the fifteenth century on, threatened and in part overpowered the eastern marches of the Empire with superior forces. In eastern as in western Europe the sense of community—of a single Christian political community of the West—disintegrated like the merest phantom on the winds of great power struggles. The old spirit of a common Western front united against the non-Christian world counted for less and less by the side of conflicts among national and dynastic power-interests.

Out of the interminable wars of the late Middle Ages, over the

Stauffer [*Hohenstaufen*] legacy in Naples and Sicily, the Angevin-Plantagenet dynasty in France, and finally even for the French crown itself, there soon emerges a new, purely secular power system. All the powers of western Europe from Scotland to Aragon share in it. If a political crisis grips one of these states, all the others are also set in motion, more or less: whether as allies or as foes, they all have an interest in the outcome. By its side there arises a multifarious system of small and medium-sized Italian states which from the first are drawn deep into the affairs of the western powers and whose own rivalries are in part determined by this involvement. The effects of west and south European power conflicts make themselves felt as far away as eastern Europe; Hungary in particular is frequently embroiled in Italian affairs. Only the north remains almost completely uninvolved. Germany, as the land at the center, only rarely fails to become involved. One comes across west German princes now in the pay of the English, now of the French, or in the retinue of the buffer-state Burgundy. The German monarchy all too frequently seeks to profit by the fierce conflicts between England, France, Spain, the Italian Guelphs and Ghibellines. For lack of comparable strength, however, the German king is generally limited to playing a subordinate role. Their dynastic interests themselves oblige the German kings of the Luxemburg and Habsburg line to divide their interests between east and west. They are thus instrumental in bringing the eastern and the western state systems in contact. Then, when at the close of the fifteenth century the Habsburgs extend their matrimonial connections from Hungary and Bohemia across western Austria (upper Rhine region) and Burgundy as far as Spain, east and west are amalgamated into one great European state system, which nevertheless does not in the least resemble the Christian community of states of the high Middle Ages. A multitude of extremely self-conscious states has appeared on the historical scene, all bent on self-determination. Every one of them seeks to extend its power as far as it possibly can, by wheatever means, fair or foul, with no regard to loyalty or faith. At the threshold of the modern era the international politics of Europe were dominated by the most Machiavellian methods—long before the great Florentine wrote his famous handbook for princes.

The great powers of the world have always made ample use of ways and means of tricking and duping their enemies. But the naive and unscrupulous way in which the great powers of the period around 1500 deceived one another has always been a source of amazement. The rich and varied experience, the mature political concepts, the firm traditions of modern Machiavellism had not yet been established. Statesmen fumbled uncertainly with pacts, pseudo-alliances, open antagonisms; they

changed allies far too frequently and arbitrarily; and they did not yet realize how greatly a state's power could be enhanced by a reputation for de-
pendability. They overextended themselves in aggressive schemes, strove
with feverish ambition for foreign conquests before the internal resources of the state had yet matured, and then had to rely on the whole
bag of diplomatic tricks which a strong and self-confident statecraft can
do without—on intrigue, bluff and delaying tactics, on being on the
look-out for lucky breaks. They knew their own interests, but had only
the most inadequate grasp and appreciation of the interests of foreign
courts. They were astute enough to see through the diplomatic maneu-
vers of others, but at the same time they were so naive as to expect the
others to be taken in by their own often quite gross stratagems. No
vow, no marriage or promise of marriage was too sacred to be heed-
lessly broken for changing political requirements. Yet ever and again
new political alliances were founded on vows and plighted troths:
engagements of one and two year old princesses were not unknown—
even engagements in advance of princesses yet unborn. Vast sums were
wasted in bribing influential statesmen at foreign courts, on lavishly
staged meetings between princes, on the dispatching of renowned "ora-
tors," despite the repeated experience that all such efforts were of no
avail. A very long time elapsed before it finally dawned on people that
the policies of great powers were in the long run determined by the
weight of their natural interests, nor by the whims, inclinations and
prejudices of individual personages. In fact, the courts of Europe learned
only very gradually and through bitter experience to distinguish between a state's genuine interests and mere adventures, and to heed the
voice of rational insight rather than the caprice of princely ambition.
The legacy of the feudal age was still powerfully and variously at work
in the Renaissance period. It is no accident that only a single Renaissance state was as early as the beginning of the sixteenth century basing
its policy on systematically gathered knowledge of the tangled interests
of the great powers, namely, the merchant republic of Venice. Venice
was the first to employ the system of permanent embassies at foreign
courts. The famous final reports of its ambassadors, made upon their return home (the so-called Relations), are still one of the most valuable
sources of our knowledge of the power-relations of Renaissance Europe.

## II.  *Suppression of Feudalism in the Late Middle Ages*

The real business of the epoch, in domestic politics as well, was the
task of suppressing feudal traditions. Whoever made the greatest strides
in this direction would gain a decisive lead in power.

The authority of the medieval ruler did not rest on the material power he possessed but almost exclusively on moral factors. What had once impelled the wandering Germanic tribes to subject themselves to a leader was their confidence in the elected warrior-king's skill in war and in his uprightness. What had curbed the warlike Franks' stubborn passion for freedom was their almost superstitious respect for the supernatural powers of the consecrated royal line, notwithstanding the flagrant and monstrous vices and crimes of the Merovingian dynasty. It was the church that gave the quasi-sacred and martial kingship [*Davidskönigtum*] of the Carolingians and later imperial families its real and principal glory—through consecration, anointment and coronation. It was fidelity, not obedience, that formed the moral bond between the feudal overlord and his vassals in the age of the Stauffer [Hohenstaufen]. This fidelity was felt to be reciprocal, not one-sided; hence it included, rather than excluding, the right to resist an "unfaithful" ruler, i.e., one who disregarded the "law." For the "law," being "eternal law," was higher than the ruler's will, higher than any necessity of state. It was neither king nor people that was sovereign, but the law. The highest task of constituted authority—strictly speaking, the only one—was the preservation of peace and justice. Something could be justified morally and politically only if it appeared to be in keeping with this supreme and proper objective: a war, for example, could be justified only if it was a "just war" of defense against flagrant "injustice." The sober realization that political conflicts can arise which pit justice against justice or injustice against injustice was foreign to medieval thought, just as foreign as the naturalistic idea of a "necessity of state" which in certain circumstances can release the ruler from moral obligations. The state itself as a suprapersonal organism, whose vitality and whose demands were by far the greatest of all, had not yet been discovered. There existed only individual rulers, princely families singled out from the mass and elevated above them, who enjoyed special privileges but also had special moral obligations. A natural force called the "power" of the state, which demanded unconditional subjection, was still unknown. There existed only the graduated rights of the ruler and his vassals. The king as the highest feudal lord was indeed the source of all positive law, that is, of the rights and privileges of his vassals; but he was neither sovereign nor all-powerful. He was, as it were, limited by the confines of his own princely prerogatives, and he shared public authority with his feudatories, especially with the great feudal aristocracy of the country (who, furthermore, had to a great extent already possessed this authority in their own right before the feudal system arose). In the feudal period the ruler did not distribute authority by assigning this or that function in public administration to this or that individual, the way the modern state appoints its officials. Instead the sum total—or at any rate the greater part—of governmental authority for a given area was transferred to a particular feudatory—more precisely, to a particular family, since the feudal regalia were no longer bestowed on an individual for life but had long ago become hereditary. Not just this or that branch of the administration was distributed, but provinces and whole counties. This was the only way in which large areas could be organized politically long before the means of transportation existed which made it possible to dominate them. But the immediate relation of the ruler to the mass of the people, i.e., to the body politic, was interrupted at a thousand points by intermediate feudal authorities. Individual churches, convents and monasteries as well as secular authorities (especially in Germany) were granted special privileges (immunities); the most diverse privileges were extended to ecclesiastical, secular and municipal corporations; all sorts of crown rights were frequently mortgaged, sold or lost; finally a kind of state-within-the state was created through the formation of alliances within the various estates (leagues, as they were called), especially between cities and among the knighthood or even among the peasantry (for instance in Switzerland). All of this served continually to weaken the bonds of the feudal polity. The ruler did not confront a uniform body of subjects, as he does in the modern state: he was merely so to speak the apex of a pyramid of rulers—princely and other vassals of the high aristocracy, ecclesiastical feudatories, municipal authorities. The "good old law" which it was his highest duty to protect and preserve consisted of the countless particular rights of the various estates.

This feudal system had of course established itself in very varying degree in the various countries of Europe. Consequently the task of suppressing it, of gathering all public power into a single pair of hands and so founding the modern state, also proceeded at a very varied pace, with differing degrees of success, and in a variety of ways. As a result the distinctive character of the several nations, in contrast to the uniformity of the feudal age proper, was already in process of formation in the late Middle Ages.

Development was particularly slow and painful in the heartland of the medieval Empire, in Germany. There both the memory of what had once been the semi-spiritual character of the imperial office, and the petrified forms of the old feudal constitution of the Empire, were in the main preserved until the beginning of the nineteenth century. As late as the eve of the Thirty Years' War the two parties of German princes, the Catholic and the Protestant, were still joining issue over their political differences in the true medieval form of a legal dispute over feudal prerogatives [*ständische Gerechtsame*]. Only in the cramped and motley world of the small and medium-sized German states, in the proprietary domains of the German territorial princes, were modern forms of government developed from the fourteenth century onwards. . . . Even so it was not until a very late date, and by no means everywhere, that these territorial princes did achieve real sovereignty, sovereignty unhampered by the legal, ecclesiastical and moral restraints and the feudalistic considerations of medieval tradition.

In the southern half of the old Empire, in Italy (in contrast to the northern half), feudal forms of government disintegrated very rapidly and completely. A comparatively modern form of royal autocracy had already been adumbrated in the Norman Sicily of Frederick II; it has been called—not quite correctly—the first Renaissance state. In the anarchic centuries of the Interregnum there then shot up on the fertile soil of urban democracy on which aristocratic feudal elements fused rapidly with bourgeois capitalist elements, a motley array of radically novel power structures—new states devoid of any traditions. The world of Italian states of the so-called Quattrocento displays a great variety of forms: the crude tyranny of warlike men of violence; the patriarchal rule of princely courts descended from the old feudal nobility, who eagerly competed with one another in providently fostering the state's economy and in enthusiastically patronizing the arts; the conservative aristocracy of patrician families in Venice, with their hereditary political sagacity; the most various forms of urban government, ranging from popular rule to clique-rule; finally the theocracy of a Savonarola and the ecclesiastical tyranny of the Papal States. Common to them all is the absence of those moral bonds of feudal fealty (or the destruction of these bonds, as in Rome during the Avignonese capacity of the church) with whose aid the monarchs of the high Middle Ages had governed. Moreover, most of them lack credentials of any kind, be they those of ancient and honorable custom, of historical antiquity, or of religious consecration. Almost all of them are upstarts who instead of possessing authority as a secure inheritance must constantly defend it against bitter enemies, both foreign and domestic, and whose states are in many instances mere temporary structures of no great historical stature. Cruel violence, deep-seated cunning and the display of a lavish pomp with which the masses are bought—these are their most important means of asserting themselves. A new self-awareness and a new self-confidence in man as an earthly creature awakened in this environment, a passionate delight in the beautiful splendor of this world which impetuously sundered the penitent piety of the Middle Ages; a spiritual world arose

which was ennobled by close contact with the treasures of classical antiquity and by the renewal of Greek ideals of beauty. The splendid
beauty of Italian Renaissance art and literature makes us forget the
world of bloody horror and human depravity within which they flowered. They also serve to glamorize the historical picture of the political
world of that period. But the political importance of the Italian states
must nevertheless not be exaggerated. Nowhere can one discern a direct
impact of the Italian model on the internal development of the other
states of Europe. These little Italian states were hardly the shapers of
international politics. They were rather the tools of the great powers
and the objects of their covetousness. The Italian city republics and the
states of the despots seem "modern" to us because of their carefree
vitality, their purely worldly and instinctual striving after power which
no longer acknowledges any principle of political conduct other than
expediency, or any political virtue other than cleverness and resilient
energy. But even Machiavelli, the theorist of these artful rules, saw
painfully clearly that Italy was not the country in which the modern
power-state of the future could come to fruition. The world of Italian
Renaissance states is a freak, the product of unique political conditions
and historical memories. The cradle of the great modern powers, of the
modern national power-state, is not Italy but western Europe. There, in
contrast to Italy, it grew quite naturally out of the soil of late feudalism.
     There, in the last centuries of the Middle Ages, one can already
see the decisive transformations of social and economic conditions, of
legal ideas and constitutional arrangements. The transformation of
things military was particularly important. The whole political and social structure of the feudal period had been determined by the knight-
service of aristocratic vassals: the army of knights went hand-in-hand
with the political and social status of the aristocratic professional warriors—lordship. But in the great battles between the French and the
English in the fourteenth and fifteenth centuries it was no longer the
mounted warriors alone but partly the foot soldiers who were decisive,
among them the middle-class English crossbowmen and archers. The
long spears of the Swiss peasants were the undoing of the mounted
knights of Burgundy, the proudest cavalry of Europe. The battlefield
of the future belonged to the foot soldiers drilled in Swiss style. No
castle wall was any longer an adequate safeguard against the blunder-
busses of the new artillery. War became a trade that could be learned
and that attracted lost souls from all over the world who were always
at the disposal of the highest bidder in return for payment. Mounted
soldiers too could be had for money, and princes soon got into the habit

of maintaining a standing paid cavalry in place of the cumbersome and uncertain feudal levy. The foundations of the whole feudal system began to crumble as soon as compensation in cash replaced the bestowing of landed property and the so-called money economy shut out natural economy. Political influence and wealth were now no longer tied to aristocratic property in land. The urban middle class with its great fund of money took its place as a very self-conscious third estate by the side of the clergy and the nobility. It challenged the clergy's monopoly in education and the nobility's in the bearing of arms. The more money proved itself indispensable to monarchical governments as a means of power, the greater became the influence of the middle class and particularly of the capitalists. The state's own resources—the income from the royal demesne and regalia—were as inadequate to the financial needs of the modern state as was the income from papal property to tremendous cost of centralized administration in the late medieval church. State and church both found themselves increasingly obliged to employ fiscal means of power, to drain the taxable resources of their subjects. In the process they more and more encroached on each other's preserves. With the passing of time the yield from the financial apparatus which governments had inherited from feudal times proved ever more inadequate. Hence there arose the perennial impecuniousness of great modern states which in turn became one of the most powerful spurs to the development of modern capitalism. Without the financial assistance of Genoese banks and of the great South German commercial firms Charles V would not have been able to carry on any of his wars.

In spite of all this the old personal relationship—the bond of mutual fidelity between crown and nobility—was not by any means destroyed. Feudal service continued to be owed and many of the old forms of enfeoffment continued to exist. The nobility was still taken to be the favored estate, the true pillar of monarchy. And this remained substantially the case until the eighteenth century. But as feudal military service lost its practical significance vis-à-vis the liability to taxation— a burden quite predominantly borne by middle class and peasantry—a new spirit came nevertheless to inform the relationship of ruler and subject. The ideal, almost idyllic relation of fidelity was gradually transformed into a system of very prosaic obligations which was strictly regulated by law. In the great states of western Europe the king's counselors—the heads of the great noble families, princes of the blood, seigneurs and barons—were at an early stage supplemented and even in part supplanted by groups of professional middle-class administrators most of whom were trained in law at the universities.[1] These crown lawyers saw the position of the ruler very differently than the high aristocracy did. They regarded neither historical tradition nor ecclesiastical and religious consecration as an adequate intellectual prop for the ruler's authority. They insisted on a juristic foundation and found one in the theory of contract in the law of the Roman Empire (the *lex regia*), the Church Fathers, and certain chapters of papal Canon law. According to this theory the office of the earthly ruler is founded on a (fictitious) social contract in which the governed unite to form a body politic [*stäatliche Gemeinschaft*] and subject themselves to a governor.[2] This theory of contract was later used by rebellious aristocrats and revolutionary popular leaders to challenge the divine right of kingship, to invoke the ultimate sovereignty of the people, and to limit the rights of absolute monarchy. An attempt to reduce the stature of the secular ruler's authority with the aid of this theory had already been made by the Papacy's clerical publicists in the Middle Ages: one who merely holds a commission from the people [they said] simply must not dare to compare the dignity of his office with the divine dignity of the pope. But the crown lawyers of the late Middle Ages, like the jurists of late antiquity, managed to use the ancient theory in a contrary sense: through an irrevocable contract the whole body of subjects had bound itself once and for all to unqualified obedience. This looks at first like mere scholastic theorizing. But its practical significance is far greater than that: behind this theory there lurked a wholly novel, comprehensive view of the nature of political authority. The concept of an absolute royal power of command and of complete and general subjection which the scholastic theory presupposed had in the feudal period still been quite unknown. Far more was now being demanded than attendance on the king and the fealty of a vassal—namely, unqualified obedience. Finally new and old legal ideas combined to raise the monarch's authority to limitless heights: equipped with supernatural powers, appointed by God, consecrated and anointed by the church, backed by ancient right of inheritance and the fidelity of his vassals, robed in the splendor of centuries of history and, finally, assured by the "contract of subjection" of the unqualified and uniform obedience of all his subjects—that is how the absolute monarch of the modern age made his appearance on the stage of history. The officers of the crown did their utmost, both through feudal litigation and with more modern means of accumulating financial and military strength, piece by piece to perfect and entrench the plenitude of his power.

For it was no longer the preservation of peace, law and tradition but the accumulation of power that now appeared as the primary and most urgent business of monarchy. It stood the crown in good stead that the strengthening of its power nearly always also meant the securing of domestic tranquillity and hence of the public weal. In all the major countries of western Europe—in England, France and Spain—the new absolutism was welcomed with relief by the great mass of the people, and especially by the new middle class, as a deliverance from the most fearful domestic feuds. The feudal system had outlived itself and had dissolved in an anarchy of willfulness. The monarchy was able to claim that its demands were at one with the "general interest" (the new slogan of the day). The prince's honor and reputation, the luster of the dynasty, seemed largely to coincide with the "general interest." In practice, to be sure, it very soon turned out that the former was being avidly pursued without too tender a concern for the latter.

Where "general interest" becomes the lodestar of policy, there lie the beginnings of modern reason of state [raison d'état, Staatsräson]. Rational action, i.e., action appropriate to one's objectives, becomes the first commandment. The rule of expediency is no doubt also quite capable of overcoming the moral scruples and inhibitions of legal thought. The early medieval ideas of law grow weak. The new scholastic jurisprudence inculcates the distinction between "eternal law," "law of nature," or "divine law," on the one hand, and mere positive statute on the other. The former is unalterable, untouchable; but it is now confined to the most general principles of legal thought (for instance, to the right of property, the divine origin of the church, and the like). The great mass of law actually in effect consists of mere statute, of mere particular decisions on concrete legal issues, and can be changed whenever it seems necessary. Mere tradition is more clearly distinguished than formerly from written statute; mere legal conviction is now open to challenge when it is not supported by written evidence. Uncertain tradition is replaced by general rules of jurisdiction laid down in writing; general legislation gradually comes to supplement mere particular decisions and privileges. The excessively close connection—indeed, the confusion—of law with morality is loosened; law is no longer rigidly tied to ancient usage. Room is made for the creation of new law. But of course this liberation is gained at considerable cost: the new power-state did not come into existence without countless flagrant infractions of the law, the harshest acts of arbitrary power, horrors and cruelties of every kind. Here too, and terrifyingly enough, the demonic force of power revealed itself, which follows all earthly greatness like a shadow, a shadow that grows deeper the more brightly shines the sun of success.

Contemporaries did not experience the birth of this new political temper and the slow death, or at least the fading, of the old ideals of chivalry, honor and fidelity without profound spiritual perturbation. The uneasy mood of the time, divided as it was between abhorrence and admiration, is mirrored most graphically in the famous memoirs of Sire Philippe de Commines who, like many another of his class, had entered the pay of Louis XI of France as official, officer and diplomat. He describes with constant amazement how in the king's personality strict piety is combined with icy cruelty, the arbitrary temperament of a great feudal lord with the most sober sense of responsibility. The whole life of the court seems given over to wild hunting parties and perpetual military expeditions, and yet time is found for the regular and considered conduct of affairs: for the promotion, through mercantilistic measures, of urban industry and of trade; for the constant enlargement of state revenue; for assiduous diplomatic activity which seeks to avert rather than to court war. The king counts no humiliation too great when he is unable to deal forcibly with foreign enemies or rebellious vassals; but at the first opportunity he takes cruel and malicious revenge, and rarely does a campaign end without captured foes being executed. No ruler of Europe possesses so grand a standing army; nevertheless he does not shrink from very ingloriously buying off an invading English army by paying a subsidy to the English king instead of expelling it by force of arms. When he needs new taxes he greets the representatives of the towns in the guise of the people's friend, the kindly father of his country; he protects the privileges of hereditary councilors against the artisans and the lesser folk; but he violates these same privileges ruthlessly when he wants to fill municipal offices with his henchmen. He binds the nobility to his service by excessive gifts of money, office and land; but no one is secure from his sudden displeasure. Suspicious as any Italian tyrant he isolates himself from his people behind the bars, moats and drawbridges of his own castle, Le Plessis. Indefatiguably he does penance, prays, creates pious foundations—none of which prevents him from misusing the church with cynical ruthlessness as an instrument of power. He takes diabolical pleasure in laying traps for refractory vassals through every kind of ruse; he invents narrow iron cages in which to tame their haughty defiance—Commines reports that the Bishop of Verdun spent fourteen years in one of these prisons. Terror, even more than real strength, is used to secure the new power position of the crown. But at the close of his reign peace has been established in the country, and all France willingly submits to the tyrant. Whether this great success has been brought about by divine providence, by the cleverness of human measures, or possibly by no more than the caprice of what the Humanists called "fortuna"—that, for the contemporary observer, is a constant puzzlement.

### BIBLIOGRAPHY *

Barbadoro, B., "Il problema politico," in *Il Rinascimento. Significato e limiti,* Florence, 1953, pp. 149–169.

Baron, Hans, *The Crisis of the Early Italian Renaissance,* 2 vols., Princeton, 1955.

Betts, R. R., "Constitutional Development and Political Thought in Eastern Europe" [1520–1559], in *New Cambridge Modern History,* vol. 2, Cambridge, 1958.

Chabod, F., *Machiavelli and the Renaissance,* London and Cambridge (Mass.), 1958 (tr. from Italian), esp. pp. 41–61.

Elton, G. R., "Constitutional Development and Political Thought in Western Europe" [1520–1559], in *New Cambridge Modern History,* vol. 2, Cambridge, 1958.

Ferguson, W. K., "Toward the Modern State," in Ferguson *et al., The Renaissance,* rev. ed., New York, 1962, pp. 1–27.

Kienast, W., "Die Anfänge des europäischen Staatensystems im späteren Mittelalter," in *Historische Zeitschrift,* 153 (1936), pp. 229–271.

Mattingly, G., *Renaissance Diplomacy,* Boston, 1955.

Näf, W., "Frühformen des modernen Staates im Spätmittelalter," in *Historische Zeitschrift,* 171 (1951), pp. 225–243.

Potter, G. R., "The Beginnings of the Modern State," in *History,* N.S. 31 (1946), pp. 73–84.

Ritter, Gerhard, *Die Neugestaltung Europas im 16. Jahrhundert,* Berlin, 1950.

Simeoni, L., *Le signorie (1313–1559),* 2 vols., Milan, 1950.

### NOTES †

[1] On the rise of a professional bureaucracy see Chabod, "Was There a Renaissance State?" (next selection).

[2] Strictly speaking this contract was really two contracts, a "social contract" proper and a "contract of government," that is, the formation of a political community and the establishment of a contractual relationship between ruler and ruled.

* Compiled by the editor.
† These are Editor's notes.

# WAS THERE A RENAISSANCE STATE? *

## Federico Chabod

*The modern state came into being in the fifteenth and sixteenth centuries, i.e., during the period of the Renaissance and the Reformation. In the following talk, the late Professor Chabod (University of Rome) makes clear how reckless it would be to read all the characteristics of the fully matured modern state back into the first phase of its history.*

I shall here do no more than put forward a few points which seem to me best suited to open up the topic we are to discuss.[1]

But first: what do we mean by "Renaissance" in respect of politics, of the State? It seems to me essential that we be specific as to chronology, so that the problem be clearly defined from the outset. In the case of most of the European States—France, England and Spain above all— we shall clearly be dealing with the sixteenth century, except for an occasional glance back to the reign of Louis XI. The same goes for the German States, though in their case it would be better to speak of the Reformation State than of the Renaissance State. But this periodization does not fit the Italian States. There we must go back at least to the fifteenth century and even further, while at the other end the second half of the sixteenth century is in Italy, much more than in other countries, already the era of the "Counter-Reformation" State—or the era of the Baroque. This latter State is no doubt very closely related to the Renaissance State; yet it displays certain novel features, and new situations and conceptions arise, with new shades of significance, which will continue into the seventeenth century.

This having been said, we can ask ourselves whether one may properly speak of a "Renaissance State," that is, of a State with a number (though of course only a limited number) of fairly distinct features.

---

* "Y a-t-il un état de la Renaissance?" in *Actes du Colloque sur la Renaissance organisé par la Société d'histoire moderne*, Paris: J. Vrin, 1958, pp. 57–74. Translated by Heinz Lubasz with permission of the publishers. The paper, having been prepared for oral presentation at a conference, contains a number of rhetorical questions, some of which have been rephrased in translation as statements. The translator has also taken the liberty of occasionally "running on" paragraphs, to give the paper a less disjointed format; and, in three instances, of putting bibliographical or incidental information into the footnotes. Nothing of substance has been altered, and nothing has been omitted.

For the Italian States Burckhardt once coined the celebrated phrase, "the State as a work of art," meaning that the State is created by the cold, clear, perspicacious will of a prince or tyrant who, just like an artist, makes a preliminary sketch and precisely calculates the means he must employ in order to achieve success. It is a very elegant formula, which has enjoyed a great vogue, particularly among historians of Renaissance civilization. But it is only a superficial formula which no one any longer thinks of applying, even to the Italian signories and principalities of the fifteenth and sixteenth centuries.

Can we then, despite diversities and despite differences in periodization, find common features, common elements of some importance, in these States of the Renaissance, not only in Italy, but in Europe as a whole? Or shall we have to relinquish the search for such a State and confine ourselves to examining the *various* States of the fifteenth and sixteenth centuries? It may well be that our search for the "Renaissance State" is at bottom no more than the desire to discover once again what has been called the "modernity" of the Renaissance, of the sixteenth century. I would want us to be very much on our guard against such an *a priori* view, against taking such a preconceived position.

If we want from the outset to discover the "modernity" of the sixteenth century (or, for that matter, of any century whatever: the remark applies generally), we shall, even without wanting to, end by coaxing the texts, without worrying overmuch about niceties—by more or less appreciably changing timbres, by imparting an eighteenth, nineteenth or twentieth-century tone to ideas, institutions, and customs which in the sixteenth century were fed by a very different spirit. Especially in the case of ideas and feelings, we would run the risk of being at least slightly off key.

I would therefore want us, in this instance as in every other, to try to see the Renaissance "State" in the spirit of the men of the Renaissance, and with their propensities; except that, once we have finished our analysis, we shall single out whatever in that State, in the political life of that period, may already be "modern." But that must be a final finding, not a preconceived notion.

For this reason I shall not dwell on the idea of nationality or on patriotism, as I do not regard them as characteristic elements of the Renaissance State—elements to which, in my view, the interpretations of, for example, Henri Hauser assign too much space.[2] First of all, because they do not constitute a general characteristic. It would in fact be quite difficult to speak of "patriotism" in the case of most of the Italian States in the fifteenth and even in the sixteenth century, excepting Florence and Venice. The "liberty" of Florence is, from the end of the fourteenth and the beginning of the fifteenth century on, exalted by Coluccio Salutati and Leonardo Bruni. The "cultural" pride of the Italian humanists vis-à-vis the "barbarism" of others does not yet amount to a "political" force. It is hardly possible to detect "patriotism"—even Lombard patriotism, let alone national—in the Sforzas' State of Milan, though it was one of the strongest and soundest.

What common bond can one find even between Florence and Venice themselves, both of which were prepared to declare themselves protectors of Italian "liberty," and to accuse each other of "egoism"? Venice also appealed to foreign powers—to France or Spain—for the purpose of breaking the resistance of the other Italian States, but, finding its hopes disappointed, it broke with the foreigners.

The self-same Machiavelli who in 1513, in chapter XXVI of the *Prince,* exhorts the Italians to rid themselves of the barbarian foreigners, and to restore Italian freedom, and in whom the Italian national spirit finds its loftiest expression, is distressed in 1509 after Agnadello, because Louis XII and Maximilian I fail to drive home their war against Venice.[3] That is altogether in the anti-Venetian style of Florentine policy; but there is certainly nothing "national" about it.

It is only after disasters, particularly after the battle of Pavia of 1525, that one can see politically oriented Italian national feeling blossom to some extent, a feeling that animates not only Machiavelli, but also Guicciardini, who strikingly sketched its development in his *History of Italy.* And besides, what was desired was not that the "barbarians" be completely expelled from every part of Italy and driven beyond the Alps (or beyond the sea, since it was now the Spaniards who threatened "the liberty of Italy"), but only that no single foreign ruler (in this case, Charles V) become *lord* of all Italy, become "monarch."

Thereafter, to be sure, during the sixteenth and seventeenth centuries, there was a whole series of works, pamphlets and discussions on the "liberty" of Italy. And the Venetian Paolo Paruta in 1579, in his work *Bella perfezione della vita politica,* exalted "this holy and venerable name, 'Fatherland,'" holding none of mankind's goods to be more precious than "the Fatherland."

But these expressions of patriotic sentiment play only a very limited role in politics, that is to say, in the life of the State. Venice has a policy of its own, and the Venetian State wants to be sufficient unto itself: there is a Venetian patriotism that is not Italian. One has only to consider Paolo Sarpi's attitude after 1606, and his political projects, in order to become convinced of this.

It seems to me that some quite analogous observations can be made concerning the German States. Here too it is enough to leaf through the correspondence of Charles V and read his appeals to the German princes, urging them to reject the French offers of alliance. There is talk "des gemainen Vatterlanndts" [of the common fatherland], of the "libertet unnd freyhait" [liberty and freedom] of the "teutscher nation" [of the German nation]—while for his part the king of France similarly appeals to the "libertés germaniques." The men who were the objects of these appeals had a political lark.

To be sure, here it was again the humanists who celebrated the glory of Germany, *den Ruhm Deutschlands,* as Wimpfeling wrote. Luther and his reformation, the German language as the language of the Bible, the polemics against Rome beginning with Hutten's: especially these things undoubtedly had an extremely profound effect. But how far does this blossoming of national feeling, which often turns into an excessive nationalism, affect the German "State," to what extent does it shape German political life?

It is a rather different story with the three great States of the West, France, Spain and England. Yet in this case too it will not do, in my opinion, *sic et simpliciter* [i.e., without further ado] to seize upon the national spirit that is already present among humanists and writers and to read it into the life of the "State." Budé's *Le Génie de la France;* the French humanists' claims for the primacy of France; "the natural affection for my Country" of which Joachim du Bellay speaks, and the "lauds of France," which "in respect of piety, religion, moral righteousness, stoutheartedness and all those rare and ancient virtues . . . has indisputably always taken first place:" to what extent did these ideas, these feelings that were voiced in cultural circles, imbue the life and policy of the State?

One is, at any rate, entitled to doubt that patriotism is already an essential force in politics, that it is already—to use Montesquieu's phrase —the "principle" by which government and the State are moved. In actual fact, from the wars of religion on, whenever one side looks for support to Elizabeth of England and the German Protestant princes, the other looks to Philip II: religious passion (or rather, religious frenzy) was a more powerful element than national patriotism. It is, in any case, among the "Politiques," after St. Bartholomew['s Eve], that we may find the first manifestation of a definite determination to transform "cultural" patriotism into "political" patriotism. Moreover, the fifteenth century had something to offer in France that the sixteenth had not: Joan of Arc obviously does not belong to the era of the Renaissance.

To summarize: in France as in Spain—for all of Spain's great "pride," which was prompted not only by Spain's power in Europe but also by the "conquests" in America—the State seems to me still to rest much more on feelings of loyalty to the king than on patriotism of a modern sort.[4] The idea of the king's sacred character is still strong enough to provide a solid moral foundation for the State, a basis later formed by national feeling and patriotism. The "nation" (and the word is in very widespread use) has not yet the political signification that it will have later on.

In monarchical regimes it is ever *honor* that is the foundation of loyalty, and it will still be so for Montesquieu in the eighteenth century.

The value of the *frontier* itself is a different one in the sixteenth century than in the nineteenth. The idea of a *natural frontier*—an idea closely linked with the "political" conception of the nation, with its geographic and linguistic boundaries—has not yet emerged: suffice it to recall the quarrel between Francis I and Henry II on the one side and Charles V on the other over Piedmont, which the French want to retain as a "rampart" of France, while the Spaniards (and certain Italians in the service of Spain) covet it as a "rampart" of Spain's Italian dominions against France. Or, again: consider the Low Countries, which certain Spaniards—the Duke of Alba among them—want to get rid of after [the Treaty of] Crespy in 1544, judging them to be of little value to Spain, but which most of them want to keep because, over and above their wealth, their geographic and military importance, etc., they are a "patrimonio tan antiguo de V. Mᵈ y stados hereditarios" ["so ancient a patrimony of Your Majesty's, and hereditary estates"], with subjects "que tienen amor y fidelidad" ["who bear (you) love and loyalty"]. The fact that they are "ancient patrimony," the legacy of distant forebears, is decisive for a Charles V and a Granvella and others besides.

We might also mention certain English designs on Calais at the beginning of the wars of religion in France: it is ever the traditional policy of the State, of the king, that is pursued, not that of the nation.

Not only Charles V's empire—that presents a clear-cut example—but the very monarchy of Philip II, with its domains in Italy and the Low Countries, divided as it was in respect of geography and nationality notwithstanding the fact that it was governed by Spaniards, seems to me much more akin to that last great multinational state that was the empire of the Habsburgs until 1918, than to the nation-state of the nineteenth and twentieth centuries.

Let us, furthermore, note the characteristic fact that there are many people serving in the administration, the diplomatic service, and even in the army, of "foreign" rulers. This is not a matter of isolated occurrences: suffice it to recall the numerous Italians who entered service and were called to high—sometimes to very high—office, be it at the court of the Habsburgs, be it at the court of France. We are here confronted, not by political nationalism, but by the beginnings of the sort of "cosmopolitanism," as one may call it, which could later find a haven only in the empire of the Austrian Habsburgs. This had already been the case with the Habsburgs in the sixteenth century; not only Charles V, with his Burgundians and his Italians, his Mercurinos da Gattinara and Granvellas and Gonzagas, but certainly Philip II as well, with his Granvellas junior, his Alexander Farneses, etc. Only: at that time this was not true of the Habsburgs alone—look at the splendid careers of some Italians at the French court. This is a fact that is thoroughly relevant to the history of Italy, which supplied a substantial contingent of recruits to that "International," not only men of letters and humanists, but also administrators, men of finance, military engineers, and soldiers. (I am touching only upon matters that bear on the general problem.)

If there are feelings that play a role in the life of the State in the sixteenth century, it is religious feelings that one must think of, rather than national or patriotic feelings. In France this applies to domestic politics only, its foreign policy having been freed from all ideology at an early stage; but with the Habsburgs it seems to be true of foreign policy as well. Political life is certainly affected by ideology, but not by an ideology of the nineteenth-century kind: in the sixteenth century it is still religion, the faith of Christ, the *respublica christiana*. It is perhaps only among the insurgents of the Low Countries that religion and national patriotism combine and become a political reality, a new *State*. Hence, in my view, it is not possible to regard national feeling and national patriotism as characteristic features of the Renaissance State. It would be anachronistic to do so. They would, in any case, be characteristic of only some countries and some situations, but by no means of all.

What of the absolute power of the Prince? Is speaking of the Renaissance State tantamount to speaking of absolute monarchy in its first phase? [5]

The Italian principalities of the fifteenth century and the French, Spanish and English [6] States of the sixteenth are indeed already absolute monarchies (I think it unnecessary to stress the fact that this absolutism is not unlimited, is not "despotism"). But let me refer at this point to M. Mousnier's very judicious opening remark,[7] that in theory monarchy had long been "absolute." So far as the Empire is concerned, it suffices to recall what was said at Roncaglia in 1158 to the honor and glory of Frederick Barbarossa: the will of the emperor is law: "tua voluntas tu lex viva potes dare, solvere, condere leges . . . rem quocumque velis lex animata geris ius est." [8]

What, then, distinguishes the *factual* absolutism of the sixteenth century from the *theoretical* absolutism of the Middle Ages which was not embodied in practice, or was so only temporarily, discontinuously, sporadically? To answer this question we must look at the State's new structural organization, that is to say, at the reinforcement, the extension, and the growing power of the corps of public officials, of the King's (or Prince's) "officers"—what today we call the "bureaucracy"— which is now in the very forefront of public life, in the *day-to-day* activity of the State.

And first: foreign policy.

Here the organization of a permanent and stable diplomacy is continued. The wealth of archives which allows us to follow the intricate play of international relations from day to day (for the Italian States from the mid-fifteenth century, for the others from the sixteenth), and which are a most valuable new source for the modern historian, these offer us clear, concrete evidence of a new fact: the appearance of a permanent diplomatic organization in the service of the State. It is the "technique" of international relations that is changing: in the thirteenth and fourteenth centuries the negotiations conducted among sovereigns, whether through personal meetings or, especially, via their agents, give no indication whatever that "a corps or a career" has as yet been established.[9] In particular, diplomatic missions are always non-permanent: they are what would today be called extraordinary or special missions. It is not until the middle of the fifteenth century, in Italy, that a permanent diplomatic service is established. This fact is so well known that I need not emphasize it. I would merely like to conjure up, as a picturesque expression of the new technique and the attitudes it called for, the scene of the discussions between the ambassadors of Charles VIII and those of the [Italian] League, in September 1495: "And on their side no one spoke but the said duke (of Milan), and on our side, one; but it is not at all our way to speak as calmly as they, and sometimes two or three of us spoke at once, and the said duke [said]: 'Ho! one at a time.'"[10]

But it is not merely a matter of "technique." As always, technical improvement, which stems from previous progress, leads in its turn to other advances. In this case, technical innovation made it possible for an activity to arise—an activity external to the State—which would have been inconceivable without it: Richelieu's "ceaseless negotiating, openly or secretly, everywhere" presupposes a permanent diplomatic service.

Parallel to the development of a system of permanent diplomacy in Europe there develops, likewise on a European scale, the principle of a European equilibrium of the powers, of the "balance of power": here too [we find that] the doctrine is first defined in Italy, from the mid-fifteenth century on, and then in France, in England, and so on. The theory of "equilibrium," which was to endure for centuries, progressively extending its geographical scope by linking, first the northern countries (in the seventeenth century) and then Russia (in the eighteenth) with western central Europe, is indeed a typical Renaissance theory. It is hardly necessary to say that the European States existed prior to the enunciation of this principle; and as a matter of fact there was, well before the fifteenth century, a system of international relations which linked the life of one State with that of the others. The asserting of this principle is what is new—an indication that the problem of international relations is assuming a novel importance of which contemporaries are fully cognizant.[11]

Let us now turn to domestic policy, to the State's internal organization.

Here too the importance and the power of the prince's "officers"—in modern terms, of the bureaucracy—is developed and consolidated. To be sure, the king's "officers" are not "invented" by the Renaissance State. Even the sale of offices, which is always laid at the door of Francis I, flourished much earlier.[12] What is essential is that the State comes to center completely on two poles: the power of the ruler and the hierarchy of "officers." The role played by the nation's estates, by the Estates General, in the life of the sixteenth-century State, is occasional rather than regular, and in reality their influence on the actual operations of government is very much reduced. It is rather the prince and the "offices" which perpetually initiate these operations. It is the rapid extension of these "offices," the multiplication of posts and the increased importance of the officials, which constitute the new reality. Richelieu noted this most succinctly, in speaking of the sale of offices: "one has to be ignorant of history" not to know that even Saint Louis [Louis IX] did not dispense offices free of charge; but it was Francis I who, "impelled by the necessities of his century, put them in regular commerce" and so became "the originator of these evil institutions."

Whether it was Francis I or Louis XII, certain it is that the "necessities of the century" increased both the number of offices and the traffic in them to an unprecedented degree, and created the "system." This is not merely a question of technique or of money. At bottom something else is involved, something specifically political, and again it is Richelieu who helps us to discover what it is.

Nothing so much enables the Duke of Guise to make himself powerful in the League against the King and his State as the great number of officers who, thanks to his influence, enter the principal offices of the kingdom;

and I have learned from the Duke of Sully that this was the most powerful motive prompting the late King to establish the annual impost [the Paulette tax on income from office], that this great prince [i.e., the king] had been not so much mindful of the revenue that he might derive from it as of the desire to make himself proof against such disadvantages, and that though the fisc counted heavily with him, on this occasion reason of State was more powerful.[13]

The strengthening of the royal administration, the multiplication of officers who paid the King for their offices, were a powerful way of keeping out cabals and political factions, and of reducing the ancient nobility, its political influence, and its chances of having men of its own in important positions in the administration.

Venality of offices, despite its very serious drawbacks, was thus of political significance. It was the equivalent, in civil administration, of the military system of hired soldiers, of "mercenaries"—a system that was also much censured, and not by Machiavelli alone,[14] though it was tied to the good and growing fortunes of the royal power which, thanks to its existence, was now no longer dependent upon the feudal nobility's monopoly of military power. Mercenary troops and officials who buy their posts form a single system comprising the foundations of the State.

I need not stress the very well-known fact that in this, too, [Italy was in the lead:] the Italian principality of the fifteenth century is already a state composed of "prince and functionaries." Miss Santoro's recent work on *Gli uffici del dominio sforzesco* (1450–1500) [*The offices of the Sforza domains*] [15] allows us very closely to examine this new type of state whose officials have very explicitly defined functions. It is worth stressing the fact that, so far as Milan is concerned, the cadre of officials does not at bottom vary a great deal over a period of more than two centuries, despite all the political changes, which from this point of view are superficial changes only. The most important reform undertaken is Louis XII's reform of the *Senate* in 1499; yet the system remains intact. Milan will pass from the Sforzas to Francis [I of France] and to the Spaniards; but the foundations of its organic structure and of its administration have already been firmly laid under the Sforzas.

There is more. Where did these officials come from? A careful analysis allows us to draw rather interesting conclusions. For in the ranks of the *ufficiali* of the Sforzas there appear members of the families which three centuries earlier had formed the dominant political group in the free commune of Milan. The de Burris, for example, gave the commune a goodly number of consuls, consuls of justice, even podestàs, in the twelfth and thirteenth centuries; in the fourteenth they continued to supply members to Milan's General Council; and as early as the beginning of the fifteenth century they appear among the "household nobility and officers resident at the court of the Duchess." In the second half of the century, these *nobili viri* furnish the Sforzas with castellans and podestàs. The same applies to the Landrino, Lampugnano, Pusterla, Settala, Marliano, Della Croce, Vimercate, and other families. (I am citing only a few examples.)

In fact, the ancient *political* aristocracy has transformed itself into an aristocracy of high officials in the service of the prince. The offices are very often and for very long periods transmitted from father to son, from uncle to nephew, etc.; even if it is not the same office, a "tradition of office-holding" is established in the same families.[16] It is not only diplomacy that attracts these ancient families and arouses their ambitions: all the offices of public administration do, sometimes even offices that are not of the first rank.

Having lost political power, which passes into the hands of the Signor—later to be Duke—the old aristocracy of the commune partially takes over the administration. This is a development which is, moreover, discernible in Florence at the time of the establishment of the Medici principate. In order to establish their power firmly and to make the Florentines forget "some of their foolishness rather than their liberty," to which the old people are so devoted (all this according to the very interesting memorandum by Ludovico Alamanni of 25 November 1516, recently published),[17] the Medici were obliged to turn to the younger people, and not only to raise them to "la cortegiana" [courtier status], habituate them to the "costumi cortesani" [customs of the court] and the "modi della corte" [fashions of the court], but also to give them offices—some in the army, others in diplomacy, others still in the financial offices, in customs, and so on.

In France, as M. Mousnier has shown, it is above all the bourgeois who come into office: there the formation of a strong royal bureaucracy comes about by a different route. The old politically powerful class, i.e., the nobility, by and large remains outside the system except for the offices of the king's household—which comes down to saying that the kingship finds its ally in the bourgeoisie. But the result is the same: the State is increasingly based on a strong and ever-growing organization of offices.

The multiplication of offices, even the sale of office and the pursuit of office, all of which are more or less familiar phenomena everywhere,[18] show us what the life of the "State" henceforth is like. These offices serve, as Richelieu said, "to keep the people to their duty." [19] The power of the prince grows, at the expense of the nobility in kingdoms such as France or Castile, and at the expense of those who mourn the loss of communal liberties in the States of the Italian princes.

But if the power of the prince grows, so does another power, namely, that of the "corps" of officials. In due course an "esprit de corps" comes into existence which, in spite of all conflicts of a personal or particular nature, binds not only the officers of justice together—the highest-ranking—but the others as well. Let us look, for example, at the investigations the king orders from time to time, to uncover abuses in the administration which are more or less everywhere denounced with great to-do. The man (or men) to whom the investigation is entrusted often, very often, runs into an impenetrable wall of silence: no one knows precisely [of any impropriety], one's colleagues are all very correct. Needless to say, this "esprit de corps" is reinforced by the simultaneous presence of father and son, uncle and nephew, by "alliances and kinships" [20] among officials. The Duke of Alba, for example, denounces abuses in Milan to Philip II in 1556; [21] and he is only repeating what has already been said by Don Juan Manrique de Lara in 1552, and what every investigation regularly uncovers.

The official is increasingly conscious of himself, of his importance, of his "office." He has a "professional" mentality which, to my mind, is of very great importance in the formation of the modern State. It is a mentality that thinks in terms of the "State" and not merely of the person of the prince: the State, which is to say, something more exalted and more enduring than the changing person of the ruler.

We may note in this connection that the word "State" itself does not acquire its modern meaning until the eighteenth century. The principle of "reason of State" is spoken of for the first time towards the middle of the sixteenth century (surely by Monsignor Giovanni della Cosa in 1547). In Machiavelli himself we find, mixed together, "stato," "dominio," etc.; the meaning of the term is not always the same, and above all it is not our meaning; his terminology is not yet the one with which we are familiar (which also applies to "nazione" and "provincia").[22] But if we consult the writers at the end of the century, we shall find the definition of reason of state "which teaches the proper means for founding, maintaining and enlarging a State" (Botero). And Richelieu speaks of: the State, the interests of the State, reason of State.[23]

This new idea of the State, the disputes surrounding "reason of State" and Machiavellism (which does not set itself the problem of good and evil), disputes whose history Meinecke [24] has traced with a masterful hand—all this is indeed also characteristic of the Renaissance State.

But let us return to the "officers." They have a conception of the State and of their own function that is already quite distinct. Here is an example: at the end of May 1544, after the defeat at Ceresole d'Alba, at a moment when funds were extremely low, Alfonso d'Avalos, Marquis del Vasto, the then governor of Milan, in the name of Charles V called upon the officials of Milan to turn over their earnings, or part of their earnings, to the Treasury to make good the deficiency. This was a habit with governors, Spanish or other: under pressure of necessity they would go so far as to pawn their wives' furs with Genoese or Milanese bankers in order to get the money with which to pay a band of foot soldiers or a Spanish regiment; only, of course, to be amply compensated by the sovereign—steady income and good fortune permitting—with pensions, fiefs and grants. "I am bound to the king by an oath of personal fidelity; I owe him my life and my possessions"—such is the sentiment of these very high personages, sprung from Castilian or Italian nobility.

But such was not the opinion of the Milanese officials. Their reply was curt and plain. We have only such wages for our offices as we deserve: they are not a bounty from His Majesty. If His Majesty and His Excellency the Governor are not satisfied with us and our work, our offices should be given to others. But so long as we hold them, we are receiving no more than what is due us.[25]

Here the feudal and chivalric conception of the public relationship between king and liegemen, between devotion and favor, comes face to face with what we may well call the "bureaucratic" conception of the State. This is a conception of "office" which constitutes a moral force. The conduct of business, everyday operations, the "technical" skill which is ever more essential to a State whose functions and interests are growing—all this increasingly reinforces this conception, and the power of the officials. If the Prince or the Governor—in short, the political head of State—is not equal to his task, the power of the officials grows excessive as they attempt to run things according to their own lights.

Allow me to cite another example drawn from the Spanish administration in Italy. In March 1542 the Marquis del Vasto wants to appoint an official with broad powers of control over the whole financial administration of Milan. The officials in charge are evidently not too keen on the proposal and try to sabotage it. They submit letters patent for the Governor's signature which define the powers of the new nominee in a way that is directly contrary to what the Marquis wants. By stealthily slipping the letters patent into the correspondence they hope to succeed. As a matter of fact, the Marquis signs at once: it is only later that he reads the text. And then, beside himself with anger, he tears up the letter and orders it redrawn in accordance with his wishes: anyone who does not like it may go. But how often the "officers" succeeded in getting their way, whether with nominations for office or with decisions of an administrative and financial nature!

Montaigne found it deplorable "that a fourth estate should be created in a polity, consisting of persons who handle lawsuits, in addition to the three ancient estates, Clergy, Nobility and People; which fourth estate, having the laws in their hands, and supreme authority over goods and lives, constitutes a body apart from the nobility." [26] But though the judicial officers are clearly the most powerful "corps," it is not they alone who constitute the new "fourth estate," but all the officers taken together. They are a real force, which prompted Richelieu on the one hand to emphasize "how important it is to prevent the officers of justice from encroaching upon the King's authority"; but which, on the other hand, made it advisable for him to avoid excessively harsh or extreme measures [against them] and made him give up his former projects for combatting the venality of offices, for fear of "some sort of upheaval." For "only with difficulty would it be possible to alter the established system for the disposition of offices, without altering the attitude [le cœur] of those who hold them; it is to be feared that then, instead of serving in no small measure to hold the people to their duty, as in the past, they might in future contribute more than any other element to disorders among them." [27]

All this seems to me to constitute an essential feature of the Renaissance State, first in the principalities of Italy from the end of the fourteenth and the beginning of the fifteenth century, and then in the great monarchies of the West. The basic element on which we must focus our attention is the growing power of the "fourth estate," allied as it is—in its political aspect—with the power of the prince, which is itself likewise growing (so that the growth of administrative centralization and of political absolutism go hand in hand).

There are, to be sure, some other things to be said. For example, the courtly ideal is elaborated, the ideal of the perfect courtier which Baldassare Castiglione caught in his Cortegiano [The Book of the Courtier], an ideal closely linked with the consolidation of monarchical power, with absolutism. It is no accident that, in the above-mentioned memorandum by Ludovico Alamanni, emphasis is laid on the need to induce the Florentines to exchange the "cappuccio" [hood of a cloak] for the "cappa" [cape]—which is to say, to adopt courtly ways and courtly garb.

One should also note the way in which the political sphere, the State and its prince, mirrors new lines of thought and shadings of form which are precisely in tune with the tonalities of the new civilization as a whole. The importance which theorists and men of action (e.g., Richelieu) alike assign to the prince's *reputation* is connected with the ever more careful fostering of "majesty," which by and by removes the prince from his subjects and sets him on a plane where one no longer dares to be familiar with him. The result is Louis XIV's everyday "majesty," a far cry from the intimate atmosphere that still surrounded even Henry IV. Protocol and Spanish ceremonial, both borrowed from the tradition of the Dukes of Burgundy, acquire an icy rigidity which puts a distance between the king and his subjects. Philip II is constantly solemn and distant, even as heir apparent, as a very young man, and will always remain so. The continual *sosiego* [serenity] of his bearing drew criticism upon him in Italy and the Low Countries from 1548–9 on.

It only remains to recall how much Baroque literature and art did to reestablish "distances" between God and man. It is no longer possible to compare God with the "maestro d'uno trafico" [head of a business firm], the way Gianozzo Manetti had done in the fifteenth century.[28] The human intimacy of the "Holy Family" in the paintings of the fifteenth century gives way to a quest for pomp and ostentation, for "majesty," of which the religious art of the Baroque is the perfect expression.[29] The Counter Reformation and the Council of Trent played their part in this development.

But I am not in a position to elaborate on these various matters which would, in any case, take me considerably beyond the Renaissance into the Baroque era. I am obliged, by lack of time and by the need to stick to what is essential for our discussion of the Renaissance State, to confine myself to the reflections I have offered on "the State constituted of offices, prince and officials."

Let me say one thing more in conclusion.

We can now try to ask the question: what, if anything, was modern about the Renaissance State?

Exactly a hundred years ago, Alexis de Tocqueville observed: "I willingly grant (administrative) centralization to be a handsome achievement, I agree that Europe envies us for it, but I maintain that it is not at all an achievement of the Revolution. On the contrary, it is a product of the *ancien régime* and, let me add, the only part of the political constitution of the *ancien régime* to have survived the Revolution."[30] I believe that we must once more take up this theme which that great historian was the first to put so succinctly.

What is the modern State? It is clearly so different from the Renaissance State in numerous respects that it would be idle even so much as to pose the question. But there is one exceedingly important element which, vis-à-vis the State that was sketched out by the Renaissance, our "modern" State has not fundamentally altered, but only enormously enlarged and strengthened. That is precisely the element of administrative organization, the formation of a "corps of officials"—of what we call a bureaucracy, which is active and powerful and constitutes the "structure" of the State. The "fourth estate" is still precisely that: I need only remind you of the example of the Marquis del Vasto in order to underline the fact that today, in a similar way, when the minister—that is to say, the *political* man—is not very competent and alert, it is the directors of the various departments who run the administration and so, to a great extent, the country.

In our time this administrative centralization, this power of officialdom, has once again increased. Even in countries like England and the United States, where local liberties—[local] self-government—so long barred the way to the "corps of officials" and their omnipotence, the last few decades have seen an increase in the authority of central government—an increase in its influence and in the number of posts, an increase in "bureaucracy." The exigencies caused by two world wars, even if, for example, it were no more than the need to intervene for the purpose of rationing foodstuffs in time of war, the intervention by the state in economic life—all such acts plainly have as their consequence an increase in the "functions" of the State and hence of the "functionaries."

And another thing. An ever more important bureaucracy is developing within the political parties themselves, especially the so-called "mass parties," with continuous, permanent organizations in which the organizational aspect plays a vital role. Anyone who wants to dominate a party today is well advised to dominate its organization first, its cadres, to have the support of its functionaries—which even fifty years ago was not the case.

This being one of the realities of the modern State, it is apparent that in this regard the State that developed during the Renaissance was a first anticipation of the modern State.

### BIBLIOGRAPHY
See bibliography for the Ritter essay.

### NOTES
[1] I wish to call attention to the fact that an analogous though not quite

identical theme, and one limited in particular to the Italian Renaissance, was dealt with at the *IIIᵉ Convegno internazionale sul Rinascimento*, held at Florence, 25 to 28 September 1952 (see *Il Rinascimento. Significato e limiti*, Florence, 1953, pp. 149–169: see especially the paper by B. Barbadoro, *Il problema politico*, and the discussion, with remarks of Prof. Renaudet).

[2] *La modernité du XVI siècle*, Paris, 1930, pp. 59ff. R. Mousnier's evaluation—"a powerful patriotism"—may also be a little exaggerated in general. Cf. *Les XVIᵉ et XVIIᵉ siècles*, Paris, 1954, p. 96.

[3] See the two letters sent from Verona, 29 November 1509 and, especially, 1 December 1509 (*Legazioni e Commissarie di Niccolò Machiavelli*, in *Opere*, ed. Fanfani, Passerini, and Milanesi, vol. V, pp. 449 and 453).

[4] On the difference between "patriotism" and a clear concept of the State, etc., see the very sound remarks by J. Huizinga, "Niederländisches Nationalbewusstsein," in *Wege der Kulturgeschichte*, German trans., Munich, 1930, p. 215.

[5] Here we revert to the discussion which M. Mousnier conducted with great acclaim at the Rome Congress [10th International Congress of Historical Sciences, 1955], which bears first and foremost on just this question of periodization. F. Hartung and R. Mousnier, "Quelques problèmes concernant la monarchie absolue," in *Relazioni* [*Reports of the 10th International Congress of Historical Sciences*, Florence, 1955], vol. IV, pp. 3–55.

[6] For England, consult the admirable recent study by J. E. Neale, *Elizabeth I and her Parliaments: 1559–1581*, London, 1953, for an account of the typical episode of Peter Wentworth's imprisonment, in 1576, for having criticized Elizabeth, and, more generally, of the queen's struggle to keep the House of Commons from encroaching on her royal prerogatives. This having been said, it goes without saying that in England forces are being repressed that already make themselves felt in the political sphere, forces which in the seventeenth century will be decisive for the country's distinctive course of development.

[7] [See note 5, above. The Editor.]

[8] ["Your will, O living law, can give laws, abrogate and establish them. . . . Whatever you, the animate law, purpose, that is law." *Monumenta Germaniae Historica, Scriptores*, XXII, p. 316. The Editor.]

[9] The remark is by F. L. Ganshof, *Le moyen-âge*, in *L'Histoire des relations internationales*, under the general editorship of P. Renouvin, Paris, 1953, p. 267. See also pp. 271–272; and G. Zeller, *Les temps modernes*, vol. I, Paris, 1953, p. 9, a volume in the same series.

[10] Commynes, *Mémoires*, VIII, 16 (éd. Calmette, III, pp. 234–235).

[11] This is the same sort of difference as that noted by W. Näf between the fact that *Herrschaftsverträge* [contracts of government] are drawn up so early as the thirteenth century, and the no less important fact that a doctrine of *Herrschaftsverträge* is not elaborated until the second half of the sixteenth century. "Herrschaftsverträge und Lehre vom Herrschaftsvertrag," in *Schweizer Beiträge zur allgemeinen Geschichte* 7 (1949), pp. 26–41.

¹² R. Mousnier, *La vénalité des offices sous Henri IV et Louis XIII*, Rouen, 1946, p. 1 ff. Richelieu had already made the observation, in his *Testament politique*, éd. André, Paris, 1947, p. 235.

¹³ *Testament politique*, pp. 233–234.

¹⁴ On this subject, see the interesting notes concerning France in G. Procacci's article, "La fortuna dell' Arte della Guerra del Machiavelli nella Francia del secolo XVI," in *Rivista Storica Italiana* 67 (1955), pp. 493–528.

¹⁵ Milan, 1948.

¹⁶ Something of a similar sort is to be met with in Mantua, though research there has not yet advanced very far. For the time being, see A. Luzio, *L'Archivio Gonzaga di Mantova*, Verona, 1922, pp. 80–81.

¹⁷ By R. von Albertini, *Das florentinische Staatsbewusstsein im Uebergang von der Republik zum Prinzipat*, Bern, 1955, pp. 362–371.

¹⁸ See K. W. Swart, *Sale of Offices in the Seventeenth Century*, The Hague, 1949.

¹⁹ *Testament politique*, p. 237.

²⁰ See Mousnier, *op. cit.*, p. 39.

²¹ Duque de Alba, *Epistolario del III Duque de Alba don Fernando Alvarey de Toledo*, vol. I, Madrid, 1952, pp. 352–356.

²² The analysis of this point in F. Ercole, *La politica di Machiavelli*, Rome, 1926, is completely sound.

²³ E.g., *Testament politique*, p. 345: "la raison d'Etat ne pourrait le permettre" [reason of state cannot permit this].

²⁴ [F. Meinecke, *Die Idee der Staatsräson in der neueren Geschichte*, Berlin and Munich, 1924 (Eng. trans., *Machiavellism*, New Haven, Conn., 1957.) The Editor.]

²⁵ A comparable situation had already arisen in September 1542.

²⁶ *Essais*, I, XXIII.

²⁷ *Testament politique*, pp. 236–237.

²⁸ A. von Martin, *Soziologie der Renaissance*, 2nd ed., Frankfurt a. M., 1949, p. 41.

²⁹ I have had an opportunity to read in manuscript a work by Prof. Georg Weise of Tübingen, which is soon to appear, and which deals with "majesty," the heroic, as characteristic of the late Renaissance and of the Baroque. In the meantime, see Weise's article, "Il duplice concetto di Rinascimento," in *Rivista Storica Italiana* 68 (1956), nos. 1 and 2.

³⁰ *L'ancien régime et la Révolution*, éd. Mayer, Paris, 1952, p. 107.

# ABSOLUTISM *

## Emile Lousse

*The nature of absolutism in its seventeenth-century form is fre-
quently misunderstood. Prof. Lousse (Louvain, Belgium), by relating
absolutism to other forms of one-man rule, indicates what it was and
what it was not.*

As it has been practiced in modern Europe, absolutism is a form
of monarchical government in which the prince's authority is in fact
free (unbound, *absoluta*) from checks by any higher authority or
organ of popular representation. It is autocracy of a type which needs
to be distinguished from other—analogous or related—forms which may
serve to support or complement it: dictatorship, tyranny, personal rule,
the centralization of power and administration. Even more important,
it should not be confused with the totalitarian State, which is perhaps
related to true democracy in much the same way as royal absolutism is
related to monarchy limited by meetings of the estates. Historically—
genetically, if one may say so—absolutism is a form of monarchy of
estates in which class distinctions have not been abrogated but the
representatives of these classes are no longer consulted. Absolutism took
pains to justify itself, first through the theory of divine right and later
through the concepts of enlightened despotism.

Absolutism is a form of monarchy. Aristotle distinguished the following: kingship of the Spartan type which, according to him, was
actually only the power of an army chief; hereditary and despotic
kingship as it existed among the Barbarians; dictatorship—elective, legal,
temporary, and by nature despotic; the Greek kingship of the heroic
age, which was hereditary and armed with extensive powers, but
nevertheless limited, all the other agencies of power being simply the
king's representatives. Tyranny which, as Aristotle always says, must
not be confused with dictatorship, is based on either force or deception;
it is but a corrupt form of monarchy. The schema is hardly new. It is
however sufficient for us to grant that the absolute monarch is in no

* E. Lousse, "Absolutisme, Droit divin, Despotisme éclairé," in *Schweizer
Beiträge zur Allgemeinen Geschichte* 16 (1958), pp. 91–106. Only the first third
(pp. 91–96) appears here. Translated by Heinz Lubasz with permission of the
editor and of the publishers.

way an oriental despot, an Athenian tyrant, or a Roman dictator. His very absolutism presupposes that law is upheld and respected rather than suspended or disdained. It is true that he is not bound by the laws of his predecessors, or even by the laws he makes himself: since he considers himself "the living law" (*lex animata*), "the fountain of justice" (*la source de toute justice*), it is always possible for him to modify, abrogate or replace what he himself ordained in the first place. But his power is not temporary, exceptional, or extraordinary; it is neither exempt from the duty of respecting the fundamental laws of the land, nor actually unlimited.

Absolutism is not necessarily "personal rule," not, at least, if by personal rule we understand a form of authority which the bearer of power exercises personally, as for example Louis XIV did after the death of Mazarin, when he no longer wanted a principal minister at all, or Philip II, the formidable *Cunctator* of the Escorial. James I of England governed through Buckingham, Philip IV through the Count-Duke d'Olivarès, Louis XIII through Richelieu, Louis XV through his favorites: all the same it is no mistake to number them among the absolute monarchs. It was on the whole the weakness of absolute monarchs to shift responsibility on to one of their entourage. No doubt only the best of them, like Louis XIV, the Great Elector, or King Frederick William I, and very few others, would have acted differently.

Absolutism does not invariably entail the centralization of power and administration. To be sure, it favors centralization and uses it, and centralization is itself consonant with its interests. But the one can exist without the other. Absolutism adjusts perfectly well to a federal State, or to a simple commonwealth with a monarchical constitution, as Spain, Austria and Prussia were until the end of the *ancien régime*. It does not call for a unitary State in the sense in which we understand it. It is not difficult to verify this, and to ascertain that the existence of centralization does not in fact coincide with that of absolutism. It is in some cases only, and even then only in a specific period, as for example in France, that absolutism and centralization advance side by side, constantly and mutually helping, supporting and reinforcing each other. Moreover, the high point of administrative centralization in France is not reached during the period of absolute monarchy at all, but after its demise. In the case of France—the most favorable example by far—royal absolutism is an important but an intermediary stage in the evolution of centralization.

Absolute monarchy is not the totalitarian State. On the contrary, the State of Louis XIV, though it was the most considerable of all the seventeenth-century States, was still modest in comparison. Though it is a State which "cannot allow that a hand be laid on the sovereign's sceptre and his authority divided" [Richelieu], yet it is a congeries of domains into which the royal authority does not venture without circumspection: the domain of private right, for example, in which the king does well not to press too hard for the codification he desires. Intervention by the central power in sectors not previously probed into becomes frequent only with enlightened despotism: education (especially secondary education), public worship, reform of the penitentiary system and amelioration of the penal law, codification, etc. The most absolute monarchies of modern times are perhaps less "totalitarian" than the most democratic of our Welfare States. They know nothing whatever of that exaltation of the people as a sort of superindividual entity in which our social—or is it sociological?—mystiques have excelled.

In a positive sense, absolutism is a form of monarchy. Monarchy itself can in our day be defined as a form or system of government in which the supreme power vests, in whole or in part, in a single individual endowed with a certain title. It has assured the equilibrium of the civilized world for two thousand years, from the triumphs of Alexander the Great to the abdication of the Romanoffs, the Hohenzollern, and the Habsburgs. The Italy of 1939 was a kingdom, not because supreme power was in the hands of a single individual, Benito Mussolini, but because its head bore the title of king. The Soviet Union, on the other hand, is not a monarchy but a republic, for the formal reason that the nominal head of State bears the title of president. There are totalitarian republics; some republics in times long past put their trust in tyrants or *condottieri;* but has anyone ever heard of "absolute republics"?

Continuing the argument—ever, appearances notwithstanding, in a positive sense—we shall contrast absolute monarchy, not with constitutional monarchy in the current sense of the term, but more broadly with limited monarchy. We shall say—we do say—that absolutism is a monarchy which once was, but does not remain, limited. It is a State derived from a common origin, and it is its common origin in the limited monarchy of the outgoing Middle Ages that will still best explain the constitutional uniformity of the absolute monarchical State of the modern era. Monarchical absolutism derives from the medieval monarchy of estates. It is a monarchy of estates in which the assemblies have been "put to sleep" by the prince's will and never meet again, so that power is henceforward exercised without their concurrence. "What pleases the prince has the force of law."

Monarchy of estates (*die ständische Monarchie, monarchie des états*) is a form of government in which the supreme or sovereign power, which belongs to the prince, is limited by the liberties granted to the various privileged orders of the community of the realm (*communitas patriae* or *regni*) and by the rights—or duties—of aid and counsel exercised by the regular representatives of the privileged orders and of the whole country. It is a monarchy in which the prince governs with the concurrence—and under the surveillance—of the legitimate representatives of the order or orders privileged by law—clergy, nobility, a third estate of bourgeois, and sometimes a fourth estate of peasants— regularly convoked into assemblies which, depending on the country, are composed of two chambers or three curias, and are variously called parliament (*parlement*), diet (and petty diet [diétine]), *Reichstag* (or *Riksdag*), Estates General (*Etats Généraux*) or Provincial Estates (*Etats provinciaux*), Stati, Stamenti, Ständetage, cortès, zemstvos, etc. This limited form of monarchy is to be found in almost all the Christian States of Europe at the close of the Middle Ages. Through a process of decomposition, or rather by predisposition, through a certain kind of evolution, the monarchy of estates managed to engender a'bsolute monarchy, which one meets with as far afield as Russia, though not in the Ottoman Empire.

The unstable equilibrium of the monarchy of estates evolved in three directions only: in favor of the prince to the exclusion of the estates; in favor of the estates to the exclusion of the prince; or else with the deliberative assemblies maintaining themselves vis-à-vis the princes, in which case the formulas of cooperation are progressively renewed. In Britain both monarch and assembly continue to exist and, despite all the crises, to maintain or reestablish a highly desirable equilibrium by drifting slowly with the course of events. It is here, and at first only here, that in the eighteenth century there arises the regime which in a little less than two hundred years has spread over the whole globe. From the rural cantons of Switzerland; from the urban republics of Switzerland, Germany, Italy and elsewhere; from the United Provinces of the Netherlands, from the federal republics of Cromwell and of the United States of America—from all these the prince is expelled: by seizing power, the representatives of the country grasp their liberties in full measure. The third and last case is that in which monarchical absolutism triumphs when the estates are put to sleep.

If I am not mistaken, the assemblies of privileged orders or estates met for the last or next-to-last time as follows: in the kingdom of Aragon in 1592, in France in 1614, in the Spanish Netherlands in 1632, in the kingdom of Naples in 1642, in Sardinia in 1699, etc. From these final or penultimate meetings on, monarchical absolutism carried the day. To be sure, it did not abolish the social hierarchy or even challenge the right of representation: it took the line of least resistance, and the monarch painlessly got accustomed to governing without a bridle: *ex legibus absolutus, absolute.*

"The king in his councils, the people in their estates." This formula, admirably balanced as it is, proved to be rather difficult to apply. How often did not the most well-meaning and long-suffering princes run up against the ill-will, blindness and obstinacy of the lowliest townsman in an immense empire, even when they were carrying out most useful or urgent tasks under the threat of imminent invasion or public catastrophe. Charles V, master of the world, confronted by betrayal at Térouanne or revolt in Ghent! That in countries in which the estates governed, private interest never prevailed, is as little true as that they were always swayed by the general interest. It is difficult in any regime, be it theoretically the best, and especially in extraordinary circumstances, to persuade everyone of his true interest, since the greater part of mankind are more readily guided by their passions. It may well be that the best way for a ruler to secure the interest of all is not to consult too many people too much of the time.

Unquestionably it was the silver of Mexico and the gold of Peru that destroyed the cortès of Castille and Aragon, and with them all the representative assemblies of the Spanish monarchy. The Dutch estates general drew the sweetness of their republican liberty from the Indies. Could it be that a sickly and undernourished condition is revealed in the permanence of British parliamentary government? It would seem that the spirit and the love of liberty remained more vital and alive where there was only middling wealth, or poverty: in Britain, Iceland, the Scandinavian kingdoms, Poland, Brandenburg, the Tyrol, the southern Low Countries, etc. An absolutist policy cannot long be conducted with success on a meager budget. Without material support, rebellion on the part of subjects would not be long delayed. Equilibrium results from a measure of material equality between powers, and from a sufficient degree of mutual need to make princes and estates indispensable to each other.

The absolute monarchs searched for theoretical justifications for their conduct. While they were believers, they used the age-old theory of divine right as the foundation for a form of State which some present-day Americans wish to call "the Baroque State." When, following the lead of the eighteenth-century *philosophes,* they became unbelievers, they lapsed into that form of classical rationalism known as enlightened despotism. They rejected the theological foundation while trying to preserve the absolute character of their power. The revolution they thus unleashed went on without them, against them, at their expense, to the proclamation of national or popular sovereignty.

**BIBLIOGRAPHY**

Clark, G. N., "The Social Foundations of States," in *New Cambridge Modern History*, vol. 5, Cambridge, 1961, pp. 176–97.

Hartung, F., "L'Etat C'est Moi," in *Historische Zeitschrift* 169 (1949), pp. 1–30.

Hartung, F., and Mousnier, R., "Quelques problèmes concernant la monarchie absolue," in *10th International Congress of Historical Sciences, Reports,* vol. 4, pp. 3–55.

Hausherr, Hans, *Velwaltungseinheit und Ressorttrennung vom Ende des 17. bis zum Beginn des 19. Jahrhunderts*, Berlin, 1953.

Hill, Christopher, *The Century of Revolution*, Edinburgh, 1961.

Just, Leo, "Stufen und Formen des Absolutismus: Ein Ueberblick," in *Historisches Jahrbuch* 80 (1961), pp. 143–159.

Kraus, Karl, "Die absolute Monarchie und die Grundlegung des modernen Staates," in *Geschichte in Wissenschaft und Unterricht* 8 (1957), pp. 257–271.

Palm, F. C., "The Rise of French Absolutism," in *American Historical Association, Proceedings: Report*, 1942, vol. 3, pp. 287–296.

# ENLIGHTENED DESPOTISM *

## Georges Lefebvre

*Did despotism become less despotic when it became "enlightened"? How much effect did the Enlightenment really have on the actual practices of rulers in the eighteenth century? These are the main questions to which the late Professor Lefebvre (of the Sorbonne, Paris) here addresses himself.*

# I

The term ["enlightened despotism"] dates from the eighteenth century. But it meant one thing in the thought of physiocrats and

---

* Georges Lefebvre, "Le despotisme éclairé," in *Annales historiques de la revolution française* 21 (1949), pp. 97–115. Translated by Heinz Lubasz with permission of the editor.

philosophes and another in the practice of rulers, and even today the concept is frequently obscured by this difference.

"When the savages of Louisiana want some fruit," wrote Montesquieu, "they cut down the tree and pick the fruit. *That* is despotic government." So be it. But as a matter of fact man's willfulness is tempered by self-interest to the extent that he becomes a rational creature. The slave-owner who possesses a batch of human beings by the same title as his domestic animals may dispose of them at will; yet he restrains his caprice in order to make the most of his resources. In feudal times a lord who was capable of reflection would realize that if he treated his own peasants with moderation he would attract fugitive slaves, and that if he gave the inhabitants of a borough their freedom, if he created a free town or guaranteed that the merchants who frequented his fairs would be free from molestation, he would increase his revenue. In this sense enlightened despotism is very deep-seated and—again as Montesquieu said—is rooted in the very nature of things.

To confine ourselves to western Europe: from the time that States were formed out of feudal chaos, kings directed their efforts towards concentrating all forms of authority in their own hands. They organized public services that were as uniform and as systematic as they could manage. From their own domains they gathered the wherewithal to maintain an army which with the help of diplomacy would allow them to pursue the proprietary dynasty's supreme objective: expansion. One may suggest that the renaissance of the State really became noticeable when taxation reappeared, and the loan was eventually added. To this end it was necessary that specie not be too scarce. It was no accident that, with the reversal of the balance of trade between Islam and the West, the re-introduction of taxation in sixteenth-century France was preceded by the rebirth of the minting and circulation of gold. . . . Precious metals were nevertheless drained off, mainly to pay for the luxury goods which the court and the ruling classes increasingly craved, goods that came from the East and, at this time, from Italy as well. It was certainly fitting that rulers should foster trade which would yield taxable wealth; but they soon thought to promote domestic manufacture which would make it unnecessary to import goods and would eventually lead to exports instead. Louis XI in particular did so, and not without success.

Although the primary goal of this policy, which was aimed at ensuring the economic independence of the State, was to increase the power of the ruler, it also provided work for his subjects and profits for the bourgeoisie. At the same time the submission of the feudatories, the establishment of domestic tranquillity, and the instituting of royal justice and police promised security to the members of the third estate and their productive activity. All this was an adumbration of enlightened despotism, and merely one aspect of the general development of European civilization: the rebirth of the State in a unified territory capable of sustaining its authority, and with it the growth of nationality; economic development, which the State protected by its very existence, but without which it would have been unable to develop its administrative and military structure; the birth and growth of a capitalism which was for a long time commercial but later became industrial, together with the rise of a new class—the bourgeoisie— which by its every interest was linked with the royal authority. King and bourgeoisie were two revolutionary forces in tacit alliance, bent on destroying feudal society, the one secretly menacing it with the leaven of money, the other dismantling its seigneurial ramparts. In some respects Louis XI looks like a bourgeois king.

The revolutions of the sixteenth century precipitated and defined the course of evolution. The Counter Reformation had its counterpart in the spirited reaction by the temporal power against aristocratic insubordination and popular ferment. In France this led to the absolute monarchy of Louis XIV, who by making the intendants into a general institution unquestionably furthered administrative centralization and rationalization. His monarchy long remained a model for continental rulers. At the same time the great maritime discoveries were giving the economic factor an unprecedented importance. First, as the hegemony of Spain was sustained by the influx of precious metals from Mexico and Peru, her rivals became obsessed with the accumulation of bullion. Then traffic with Asia and the colonial exploitation of America gave commercial capitalism a tremendous boost. The bourgeoisie applied part of its profits to industrial production, which became concontrated and thus susceptible of rationalization. Manufacture continued to need the protection of the State, which for its part was determined to subordinate industry to its own bullionist aims. A doctrine was worked out—mercantilism—which strengthened this bond, and which found in Colbert so remarkable an administrator that "Colbertism" became synonymous with it. The remarkable effectiveness which Louis XIV's army eventually achieved, and consequently the Great King's conquests, were without too much reflection attributed to this system. It goes without saying that the results did not seem entirely satisfactory to the men of the early eighteenth century. Not only were they extraordinarily worried by the king's power; it was also clear that his arbitrary power often set his private whim above the interests of the State properly understood. Wastefulness, the construction of sumptuous edifices, wars of prestige, and the lamentable consequences of the revocation [of the Edict of Nantes], all aroused anxious thoughts.

## II

These traits did not tally with the picture of the ideal king of Salente [1] which Fénelon drew in his *Télémaque*. In point of fact the Christian conception of the prince's duties was in principle different from his. Medieval theologians had not confined themselves to recalling the prince to the obligations of religious morality. Appealing to common sense, they had made bold to construct a natural law which explained the phenomenon of society and its governance in terms of a social contract among its members, and tacitly enjoined the sovereign to govern only to the benefit of the community. This idea, so remote in origin from the enlightened despotism of eighteenth-century laymen, was at variance with the exceedingly bold realism of royal practice. But it did not go beyond moral exhortation, and saw man's goal as salvation in the next world, not as well-being in this.

Modern rationalism, which was founded by Descartes in the seventeenth century and took two centuries to work out the concept of positive knowledge, did not rule out this way of looking at things; but it gradually restored to earthly existence an importance which, to be sure—and this goes almost without saying—it had never lost in the daily thoughts of most men. Descartes established that the phenomena of the perceptible world, of "nature" and of "matter," invariably followed laws, and that reason, by discovering these laws, supplied the means by which they could be turned to man's advantage. He relied above all on mathematics. But the eighteenth century was persuaded by certain English doctrines, especially Newton's, that only observation and experiment could confirm the accuracy of the results reached by reason. Through association with empiricism, therefore, rationalism became experimental. Descartes did not apply his method to economic life or to politics because human conduct in these spheres, being condemned to contingency by free will, did not seem to him to lend itself to the formulation of absolute and eternal truths. But physiocrats and philosophes came to believe that, like nature, economics and politics admitted of discoverable laws—one need only recall, once again, *The Spirit of the Laws*. The fundamental maxim of rationalism, "To know the world in order to be in a position to change it," thus took on its full meaning. It followed that inquiry must be free. At the same time the critique of mercantilism and of arbitrary government, and the interests of the bourgeoisie, came to the same conclusion in the name of social utility: *laissez faire, laissez passer;* abolish serfdom and respect the individual; give up intolerance, which deprives you of the blessings of concord; suppress privilege in favor of civic equality, and recognize that merit alone justifies admission to positions of leadership in both society and the State; if you do, individual initiative and competition, stimulated by the lure of profit, will bring with them universal prosperity and culture in the greatest possible measure.

How were these reforms to be brought about? The English revolutions [of 1642–9, 1688] had assigned the task of reform to the constitutional regime. But though Locke had become the prophet of liberty for all Europe, justifying it by the appeal to natural law, physiocrats and philosophes had no notion, at least until Rousseau, of similarly invoking the social contract, or of advocating the adoption of British political institutions—not excepting Montesquieu, for all that he praised them. It seemed to them that the king's authority was indispensable to the creation of the new world. Only a despot, being omnipotent, seemed to them capable of setting the ignorant and hide-bound masses on to new paths. What was essential was that the despot listen to the physiocrats and philosophes, that he follow the natural laws they had discovered, that he accept the rationalist conclusions they had formulated—in short, that despotism become *enlightened*. Henceforward the ruler, subordinated to law and social utility, was to cease being the proprietor of the community and to become the first of its servants. This idea had no force so far as Holland was concerned, where the upper middle class governed, or England, where in conjunction with the aristocracy it governed in agreement with the king. But it did apply to those continental States of western Europe in which the bourgeoisie was by law kept in a subordinate position and was excluded from power, and was now becoming aware of its strength though it could see no opportunity of emancipating itself and was not bold enough to seize one.

## III

The enlightened despotism of physiocrats and philosophes offered sovereign rulers suggestions that were compatible with their traditional policy to the extent that they judged them likely to promote the enrichment of their states and to increase their power. But they found them no more acceptable in principle than the prescriptions of the theologians. It was not proper for an absolute monarch to stoop to promulgating "laws of nature." It is totally unrealistic to imagine that they set aside their personal whim in favor of the interest of the subject. They were already busy keeping the aristocrat in line, and therefore had no intention of raising the bourgeois to their level. Pride of caste forbade such a step, for the monarch regarded himself as the premier gentleman of his kingdom; prudence counseled against it even more strongly, owing to the fear of once more arousing rebellion or, given a docile aristocracy, of falling prey to popular ventures. A few ministers and a slightly larger number of their subordinates were indeed won over to the new spirit. In France especially it helped to create a body of competent, experienced administrators with a taste for innovation who, like Turgot in Limousin, took the initiative in making technical improvements and decried the shackles laid on them by the mass of privileges and the innumerable malformations of the administrative machinery. In France in the second half of the century the government gave up religious persecution, showed a degree of forebearance to writers, and manifested some leanings in the direction of economic freedom. Some improvements in detail were also achieved in Italy, notably by the Habsburgs of Tuscany, and in Spain, though the latter was not exactly hospitable to toleration and the Inquisition even continued its rampage. In any case, in France attempts at more extensive reform always foundered on the resistance of the nobility. Elsewhere, the redemption of seigneurial rights imposed on the peasants by the king of Sardinia was a remarkable exception.

All these states were Catholic. It was one of the distinctive features of this period that the religious orders were comparatively out of favor in France, as is shown by Machault's edict concerning mortmain and by the commission of the regular clergy—and that the Jesuits were suppressed, first in Portugal and then by the Bourbon rulers, who forced the Papacy to abolish the Society of Jesus. Indifference or hostility towards the clergy, indeed even towards Catholicism, undoubtedly inclined a part of public opinion to welcome such measures. But, apart from the fact that they in no way implied an intention on the rulers' part to secularize the State, one must bear in mind that Colbert's utilitarian mentality had little use for monks; that kings were disputing the Papacy's supremacy over the temporal power, and that on this count the Jesuits, who were regarded as the representatives *par excellence* of ultramontanism, aroused distrust and censure in the royal administration and above all among members of the *parlements*. The attitude of the Catholic despots was in fact merely one facet of that caesaropapism of which the Civil Constitution of the Clergy furnished an extreme interpretation: the Church is within the State, not the

State within the Church; the State has the right to regulate the Church in all matters not pertaining to dogma.

All in all, governmental practice in the eighteenth century did not differ in principle from what had gone before. Up to a point it adapted itself to the new ideas which economic and social evolution favored. As it became "enlightened"—if one wants to speak this way—despotism strove, with more or less vigor and success, to strengthen the power of the State, that is, of the monarch. The social structure was in fact transformed by the rise of the bourgeoisie, but the philosophes' propaganda failed to change the law. As a result the philosophes did not think that their conception of enlightened despotism had been fully carried out in the West, particularly as the above-mentioned reforms often lagged. This partly explains their mistaken belief that they had succeeded in converting the rulers of central and eastern Europe.

## IV

Owing to their distance from the Atlantic, the central and eastern regions of Europe had not taken part in the maritime and colonial boom at all, and felt its effects only slowly. With every step beyond the Elbe and down the Danubian basin the lag became more evident: an often sparse population of servile peasants, uncultivated expanses and wild forests, few artisans, and a small middle class concentrated in the larger ports and in the towns with famous fairs. The noble landlords' proprietary and seigneurial rights remained unimpaired. In the seventeenth century the kings, who lived mainly off their own domains, possessed neither a modernized administration nor a modernized fiscal system and, as a result, no regular army. Their states, which had no natural frontiers, seemed as if moving or unstable on the vast plains. Distance, and the meagerness of their resources, protected them from western covetousness; but they all stood in fear of one another and did not rank as major pieces on the chessboard of Europe. Nevertheless, thanks to the determination of a number of sovereigns, two of these kingdoms emerged from obscurity. In Prussia there were three successive Hohenzollern of very unequal talent, whose sustained efforts gave rise to a tradition of government which Frederick II inherited, continued and perfected. In Russia there were Peter the Great and, much later, Catherine II. In creating a State out of nothing, following the western example, these personages showed by their success what a despot could do when, at least to a great extent, he subordinated his private life and his private pleasure to his primary duties, and when, obliged as they were to develop the wealth of their domains in order to supply themselves with the wherewithal of action, they fostered the belief that their subjects' lot was their greatest concern, when in fact, like their western counterparts, they were intent only on increasing their own power.

The least arduous task fell to the Elector of Brandenburg, who was soon to be king of Prussia. His territory was not very large and the domains of the crown occupied about a third of it, so that the ruler's influence could make itself felt very effectively. The population, which was entirely German to begin with, was easily able to germanize the immigrants who in addition, having fled persecution and poverty, looked on the new master who gathered them in as their benefactor. The feudatories, whose forebears had wrested these regions from the Wends and Balts, were quick to yoke themselves to the service of the ruler. Whatever was left in them of the discipline of the conquering colonist undoubtedly contributed to their submissiveness. Besides, they did not all consider themselves rich and were obliged to find employment for their sons: the king's bread, they said, is always good. Although the duchy of Prussia remained outside the Empire, the Electorate of Brandenburg was part of it, and the Hohenzollerns' subjects shared in German culture: the universities supplied able administrators. Via Germany, finally, the Prussians came in contact with Austria, where Spanish institutions were not without influence; with England, where the Elector of Hanover became king in 1714; and above all with France, whose Sun King caught their imagination. Rationalism reached them: it was at Halle that Wolf adapted Cartesianism to the German mind, and that the *Aufklärung* in the middle of the eighteenth century became the philosophy specifically of the officials, pastors and professors of the Kingdom of Prussia. These men, who were schooled in temporal obedience by Lutheranism, who were paid by the ruler, who lacked the support and stimulation of a vigorous bourgeoisie, these men brought rationalism into harmony with the policy which natural conditions and circumstances imposed on the Hohenzollern: the sovereign, who was himself the servant of the State, was entitled to submission as the paternal teacher of his subjects; the *Aufklärers'* task consisted in assisting him by morally improving their compatriots, largely via the pastors, whose doctrinal teachings became ever more latitudinarian as a result.

In their eagerness to acquire population, the Hohenzollern made toleration a fundamental principle of their policy from the time of the Revocation of the Edict of Nantes. They colonized vacant regions; from Austria they borrowed the cameral system of administration which came from Spain; from France they took over mercantilism and undoubtedly also the system of a drafted militia which had been introduced by Louvois; later on, in the days of Frederick II, they also introduced the general tax [ferme générale]. Their efforts were directed towards the creation of an army. So successful were they that they attained an importance which, by the standards of the time, was out of all proportion to the size of their territory and the total strength of its population. Frederick II followed the same course, and under his direction the Prussian State achieved its ultimate goal—expansion. His victories began to seduce the other Germans, and he himself became, for public opinion and for a number of sovereigns, a model ruler.

Circumstances were far less kind to the tsars. Their immense empire seemed to be boundless, and the population was sparse except in the Moscow heartland. The north, the Urals, and Siberia, offered enormous scope for colonization. Catherine added the steppes that stretched to the Black Sea, whose immense wealth awaited exploitation. Thanks to the vast extent of the territory, distance actually worked against colonization, as it did against administrative centralization and military undertakings—an obstacle which the Europeans of the west did not fully appreciate. In the last analysis, the tsars' principal capital was human beings: they lacked raw materials, technical skills, and financial resources. It was, moreover, far more difficult for Russia to have recourse to the West than it was for Prussia. For Russia, Germany was an indispensable intermediary. The dynasty itself sought family alliances there, and it was a German woman who carried on the work of Peter the Great. In this connection the Baltic provinces, which were dominated by German feudatories, played so important a role that the latter infiltrated the personnel of government. One of the features of Russian despotism was none the less a stubborn determination to put the ruling class to school with the West, that it might serve the State more effectively. It took a great deal of time to accomplish this, and even so the benefits to administration and economy, if not to the diplomatic and military services, never matched those achieved by the Hohenzollern.

The tsars nevertheless followed the same course. They kept their Russian subjects within the bosom of Orthodoxy, but adopted a policy of toleration towards the varied populace of their empire and towards immigrants. They adopted mercantilism, created state industries, and took private enterprises under their wing. Administrative services were organized by and by. The serf population furnished lifetime recruits. In contrast to the Hohenzollern, the Romanoffs did not succeed in balancing their budget. They borrowed money from England to no better purpose than to issue a paper currency. Peter the Great's and Catherine's annexations; the dismemberment of Sweden, Poland and Turkey; the Treaty of Teschen, by which Russia jointly with France guaranteed the constitution of the German Empire; intervention by the League of Neutrals in the American war—these were held by public opinion to have crowned the work of the Russian despots as the successes of Frederick II crowned the work of the kings of Prussia.

Having lost Siberia [sic: Silesia], and being alarmed by Russian advances in Poland and Turkey, the Austrian monarchy in its turn decided on renovation, Maria Theresa with cautious empiricism, Joseph II with implacable obstinacy. Austria too shared in German culture: the Aufklärung "enlightened" her officials—the Kameralisten like, for example, Sonnenfels—as it did the Prussians. They were likewise affected by the teachings of the physiocrats and the English economists. Joseph II revamped the administration from top to bottom, following a rigorously uniform, centralizing plan in which French influence is apparent. His mercantilism reverted to the virtual prohibition of imports. Finally he decreed the complete overhaul of direct taxation. His reforms differed from those of his rivals not only in extent and generality: the Habsburg monarchy being Catholic, Joseph was led to adopt the Latin despots' attitude towards the Church in an equally radical form. On his own authority he overturned its institutions and even its liturgy; the secular clergy became salaried officials, and the regular clergy was substantially reduced; the Pope was treated with deference but got nothing. Joseph carried toleration a good deal farther than the other Catholic rulers: the Protestants saw their civil rights recognized and were admitted to public office.

The enterprise came to a bad end. The Habsburg domains presented a diversity which proved irreducible because its various constituent elements vigorously resisted centralization: Lombardy and Belgium because they were attached to their own, western civilization, Hungary and Bohemia because they had a deep-rooted historical tradition. Resistance was all the fiercer because Joseph, though he neither prohibited the use of local languages nor had the least intention of germanizing the populations, made German the official language as a mark of administrative unity. Had foreign affairs been as kind to him as to his rivals, he might have succeeded. But he came to grief in Bavaria and in his dealings with Holland. Then, having allowed Catherine to draw him into her Turkish campaign, he became entangled in a disastrous war which allowed opposition among the Belgians and the Hungarians to burst into open rebellion. He suspended his fiscal reforms and, after his death, his brother Leopold intensified the retreat. But administrative and military reforms were retained, and until 1855 the Habsburgs' ecclesiastical policy also remained faithful to "Josephinism."

## V

In our view, then, the work of these rulers, seen in historical perspective, marks the extension of western civilization to the East. In creating the State, adopting rationalist methods in administration and economy, and forming modern armies, their work exhibits a facet of western civilization. Its originality lies in details of adaptation and in the rapidity with which the work was carried out, though this last fact is to a considerable extent explained by their having borrowed models which had already been slowly worked out by the older monarchies.

It is only proper to add that their work also contributed to the diffusion of other elements of western civilization, to the formation of an aristocratic cosmopolitanism in which the language, literature, art and fashions of France were generally preeminent. Conversely, the influence of rationalism, which the *Aufklärung* reduced to utilitarian precepts that were often very matter-of-fact, was helpful to despotism and gave it greater standing in public opinion. As in the West, the need to obtain recruits for administration and economy, and to protect and stimulate the nascent capitalism, led rulers to ally themselves with the bourgeoisie and to encourage its growth. "Enlightened" despotism was, as elsewhere, an intermediate stage between arbitrary tyranny and bourgeois monarchy.

For a long time the philosophes praised it almost without stint. Since they were concerned above all with intellectual freedom, they valued religious toleration, the comparative freedom granted to philosophical speculation, and the favor shown to scientific research. Frederick II appeared to adhere to their banner. In his correspondence and conversation he showed his contempt for German culture by using French, and he remained impervious to religious sentiments. Catherine too appeared to be an adherent, notably in drafting the instructions for her famous Commission of Reform. The Prussian officials and the *Kameralisten*, the professors, pastors and writers of stories, were even more captivating, inasmuch as the sincerity [of their conversion] seemed less circumscribed by caution. Montesquieu and Voltaire would have written endless eulogies had they known of the project for a code of law which Carmer prepared for Frederick II and submitted to his successor, Frederick William II. This code declared the ruler to be subject to the law, guaranteed individual liberty, and provided specific guarantees against the arbitrary dismissal of judges and other State officials.

In reality, the humanitarian declarations were nothing more than *jeux d'esprit* so far as the rulers were concerned. What they were essentially interested in was the growth of their power, and they took care to separate what could be of advantage to them from what was best forgotten. Joseph II, who because of his zeal for innovation was thought to act from intellectual conviction, was particularly distrustful of the philosophes. Having remained a good Catholic, he had no desire to see Voltaire at the time of his visit to France. So far as Frederick and Catherine were concerned, a well-disposed public opinion was politically useful: when they were thwarted by the alliance between France and Austria the philosophes' praise of them, which helped to make the alliance more unpopular, was not to be disdained.

If the vanity and the interests of the philosophes contributed to their lending themselves to this sort of use, so did their passion for pamphleteering. They did their utmost to indoctrinate their own rulers and to confound the clergy, but with only moderate success. Hence they took the greatest delight in contrasting the monarchs of the West with the potentates of the East. The philosophes did not point out that a policy of toleration was easier for Frederick and Catherine, who were at some distance from Catholicism and were the heads of national Churches. Nor did they stop to think that it is the will to power, and natural and historical conditions, which govern the conduct of rulers, and not the propaganda of philosophers or a solicitude for human progress.

## VI

One notes with surprise that the philosophes do not seem even to have realized that Frederick's and Catherine's social policy showed itself no whit less conservative than that of the lords of the West. As their interest in the condition of the peasantry and of the town "rabble" was slight, the philosophes were not disturbed by the fact that enlightened despotism did these groups very little good. Frederick II's mercantilism in particular scarcely ameliorated their condition, since it was geared to exportation rather than to domestic consumption. Poverty in the towns was no less great in Prussia than in France, and beggars and vagabonds in the countryside were no fewer. At the very least the condition of the bourgeoisie might have given them pause. The members of the bourgeoisie got some concessions in return for their services: they were given some subordinate posts, and anyone who distinguished himself through exceptional service even got a title; they were formed into privileged bodies in the towns, were exempted from military service, and were granted capacity to acquire lands or serfs by individual title. For all that, the bourgeoisie remained in a subordinate position. As a rule, landed property remained the monopoly of the nobility, and as a matter of fact the same was largely true of high administrative office and military command. The most serious grievance was undoubtedly of an economic order. Though the capitalist entrepreneur felt the benefits of protectionism, individual initiative was none the less curbed, and not by regulations alone. In Prussia, in order to ensure collection of the excise, the king prohibited manufacture of and trade in taxable goods outside the towns. In Russia, where the peasants were the serfs of the crown or of noblemen, the bourgeois might not employ them without a permit. In the West, it was through the exploitation of rural handicraft—underpaid and exempt from corporate supervision—that commercial capitalism collared the working class: much so-called "industry" was simply the management by an urban merchant of domestic workers scattered in villages. By hampering this sort of development the new monarchies both impeded the rise of the bourgeoisie and unwittingly jeopardized their own economic work.

The enlightened despots [of central and eastern Europe] conceived of the social structure the way their western rivals did. The nobility seemed to them especially suited to supply the best assistants. Peter the Great had tied them to the service of the State by means of the *Chin*.[2] Frederick II thought that as a rule his officers should belong to the nobility. His predecessors, who had been concerned with subjugating the nobility, had looked on it with suspicion; but as by Frederick's time it had become docile, it won his trust. He left the nobility a great deal of autonomy: the *Landrath* [sheriff] of the *Kreis* [county] was a local nobleman whom his peers presented to the king for confirmation; where provincial estates [i.e., parliaments] existed the aristocracy itself governed. Frederick even assisted the Junkers financially by organizing mutual mortgage loans in some provinces, though it did not occur to him to offer similar benefits to the peasants.

Catherine II tended to be even more conciliatory [towards the nobility]. She knew that, because of her German origin, she was suspect on the grounds of nationality. Everyone knew from history and from her own example—after she had dethroned her husband and either ordered or authorized his murder—that noble conspiracies and, if need arose, assassinations, set limits to the tsars' authority. Whereas the German rulers, who were secure in their legitimacy, exercised their despotism with austerity and severity, she looked to favoritism as a guarantee of her security. But she also treated her nobility with consideration. In the end she promulgated a charter by which they were formed into special bodies within each district, with assemblies and elected officials, and with special courts of law for their members. It was thus by tacit compromise that the enlightened despots won the compliance and cooperation of the aristocracy.

But the most characteristic feature of this understanding [between ruler and nobility] was that it was the peasants who paid the price for it. Historians have noted that in Prussia, as in Poland and Russia, *Leibeigenschaft* (servitude properly so called, which reduced the peasant to slavery) was the exception. As a rule, the rustic was an *Unterthan* [subject] and, being thus regarded as the king's subject, had access to his courts. This was in fact an illusory guarantee: the *Unterthan* was subject to seigneurial jurisdiction. The Junker had the right to inflict corporal punishment on him at his discretion; it was via the Junker that the king collected his taxes. Many peasants had no holding, but only a patch of ground held by a precarious title. Ordinarily, the *Bauer's* [peasant's] own tenure was not hereditary and he could not dispose of it freely. The Prussian landlord had extensive domains under direct cultivation, and he showed himself only too ready to add holdings from which he evicted the peasants. Not only did the *Unterthan* owe ground-rent: he also found himself being subjected to arbitrary labor service for the cultivation of the landlord's own domains, and forced to send a stipulated number of his children to the manor to serve as menials—*Gesindedienst*. Finally, he might not ply a trade without permission from the lord, who reserved for himself not only mill and forge, but brewery and distillery as well.

Frederick II was quite convinced that the economists were right in demanding that the peasant be liberated and turned into a proprietor or a wage-worker, since the lure of gain would ensure hard and conscientious work infinitely better than coercion could. He abolished *Leibeigenschaft* on his own domains, authorized the fixing of labor services and even their redemption, as well as that of ground-rent. But he never dared interfere with the economy of the seigneurial *Gut* [estate]. At the most, in some provinces he ordered registers of landed property drawn up, in which the peasant's obligations were specified once and for all. Yet even in this he was not universally obeyed by any means. The Prussian State was even more distressed over the eviction of tenant-farmers [*Bauernlegen*], because it affected the yield from taxation and jeopardized the recruitment of soldiers [*Kantonisten*].[3] It had nevertheless to be content with curtailed recruitment [*Bauernschutz*], and was never fully in control with respect to these decrees.

In Russia it was worse. The serf had no access to the State's courts. He could be detached from his land and his family sold or deported. On one occasion Catherine II had curbed the tyranny of some lord who had tortured serfs or put them to death. She did not do it again. She even gave numerous peasants from the crown estates, where they were supposedly better treated, to her favorites. Even worse, upon her conquest of the Ukraine she introduced serfdom there.

That compromise with the aristocracy was an essential condition for the success of enlightened despotism in Prussia and Russia is demonstrated by the counterexample of Joseph II's contrary experience. He suppressed the autonomy of the nobles through his administrative reforms, by eliminating the provincial estates and, in Hungary in particular, the cooperation of the comitats [4] and the courts. He abolished serfdom both on the aristocracy's domains and on his own. In reorganizing the land-tax he dared to fix at a set percentage of the tenant-farmer's net income the maximum ground-rent payable by him [to the landlord]. Consequently the feudatories everywhere opposed him and brought about his defeat, the most striking sign of which was the abandonment of his financial reform. In the course of the reaction which ensued upon his death, his defeat was plainly confirmed by the restoration of the nobility to its privileges.

Like the traditional policy of the western rulers (at least of those who were not lacking in realistic intelligence), from which it did not substantially differ, the despotism of the "enlightened" rulers of the eighteenth century thus harbored a contradiction: it stimulated the growth of the bourgeoisie; yet at the same time it was not wholly successful except in alliance with the aristocracy, while conflict with the aristocracy brought Joseph II to his knees and forced Louis XIV to reconvene the Estates General.

# VII

Enlightened despotism has sometimes been contrasted with the French Revolution, to the effect that the abrupt change worked by the latter was unnecessary and that the former achieved comparable results at less cost. It follows from what has so far been said that such an assertion is highly equivocal.

If one has the enlightened despotism of the philosophes in mind, one can defend the assertion on the assumption that the philosophes had persuaded the rulers to grant equality of rights at the expense of aristocratic privilege—a qualification that still leaves the assertion open to question, since not a single one of the kings made an attempt to do so. If, on the other hand, one has the enlightened despotism of the rulers in mind, which is what seems to be the case, then the assertion is sophistical in that it fails to take account of the distinction which we have just pointed out.

Confusion creeps into the discussion because the French Revolution, in one part of its work, merely completed a job which the monarchy, unable to overcome the resistance of the privileged, had left unfinished. The revolutionary bourgeoisie was able to complete national unification and to rationalize the administrative organization. Internal barriers were overthrown. The orderly division of the country made it possible to establish uniform institutions. With the suppression of privileges, all Frenchmen found themselves subject to the same law. Both enlightened despotism and the philosophes got due credit for all this, and the understanding between the monarchy and the bourgeoisie persisted. It is not surprising to find the Emperor Leopold and the [Prussian] minister Herzberg passing favorable judgment in this respect on the decrees of the Constituent Assembly: had they been able to benefit by it, their power would have increased. It is in this sense that Tocqueville ventured to conclude that by removing the obstacles that hampered the central authority the Revolution reinforced despotism.

But the French Revolution is also the advent of the bourgeoisie. Louis XVI became a constitutional monarch subordinated to an elective national representative body. The central authority itself was severely limited by the regional and communal powers given to governing bodies that were likewise elective. The philosophes' enlightened despotism was thus outdone, though if it is understood as favoring the bourgeoisie, the triumph of that class was not fundamentally contrary to its intentions and its historical significance. For the enlightened despotism of the rulers, on the other hand, it was a mortal blow. It is not surprising that, after due reflection, they condemned the Revolution and combatted it.

Nor is this all. There is yet another facet to the Revolution, one of far greater importance for the majority of Frenchmen. During the night of August 4 [1789] equality of rights acquired a resounding fame. The bourgeoisie was no doubt content with the legal principle; but the peasants were deaf to it; and the feudal class was instantly dissolved by it, not only losing its privileges but also being attacked in its social authority and in its wealth. Its losses were further augmented by the sale of clerical property and, later on, of the goods of émigrés. It is understandable that the counter-revolution should have been a crusade of the aristocracy even more than of the despots. From this point on the alliance of monarch and nobility was firmly sealed.

It remained for Napoleon to teach the rulers of the continent how to go about exercising personal power under cover of a constitution, and so to preserve for despotism all the benefits of integration which the Revolution had brought about. It likewise remained for him to remind the aristocracy that equal rights did not prevent it from retaining its favored position in the distribution of high State office, or even from reestablishing, if need be, noble rank and entailed land. Besides, in this matter the British oligarchy had long been teaching the same lesson. As the history of the nineteenth century bears out, these examples were taken to heart.

### BIBLIOGRAPHY

Hartung, F., *Enlightened Despotism*, London, 1957.

Lhéritier, M., *et al.*, "Histoire du despotisme éclairé," in *Bulletin of the International Committee of Historical Sciences*, esp. 1 (1928): "Le rôle historique du despotisme éclairé particulièrement au 18e siècle," by M. Lhéritier, pp. 601–612; 2 (1930), pp. 533–552; 5 (1933), pp. 701–804; 9 (1937), pp. 2–131, 135–225, 519–537.

Lindsay, J. O., "Monarchy and Administration" [1713–1763], in *New Cambridge Modern History*, vol. 7, Cambridge, 1957, pp. 141–160.

Morazé, Ch., "Finance et despotisme, essai sur les despotes éclairés," in *Annales*, 3 (1948), 279–296.

Pares, R., *Limited Monarchy in Great Britain in the Eighteenth Century*, London, 1957.

Walder, E., "Zwei Studien über den aufgeklärten Absolutismus," in *Schweizer Beiträge zur Allgemeinen Geschichte*, 15 (1957), pp. 131–171.

### NOTES †

[1] Country of the Salentini, in Calabria, where Fénelon set his ideal state.

[2] Literally: "rank." Peter the Great reversed the system customary in aristocratic societies: instead of promoting men in government service and in the army in accordance with their social rank and title, he made social rank and title depend on promotion in government service or in the army.

[3] So called from the system of Cantons into which the country was divided for purposes of military recruitment.

[4] The name derives from the feudal *comitatus*. The comitat was a unit of autonomous local self-government.

† These are Editor's notes.

# THE EMERGENCE OF THE DEMOCRATIC NATION–STATE *

## Otto Hintze

*The victory of the bourgeoisie signalized by the French Revolution transformed the dynastic into the national state. In the following essay, Hintze exhibits the roots of this new form of state, and the fusion of capitalism, liberalism, and nationalism within it. (Hintze's rich and penetrating analysis reveals the influence of Max Weber's sociology, and suggests how fruitful a study of sociology can be for the historian.)*

The radical ideas of popular sovereignty, democratic republicanism and the complete separation of church and state, which had emerged in the Puritan Revolution of 1649 but were not realized in any enduring form in England itself, were carried to the American colonies by the Puritan emigrants. There they formed the foundation of the United States Constitution, a thoroughly modern structure which came into being in a new country that knew neither hierarchical nor feudal traditions. The extensiveness of this new oversea realm ruled out from the beginning the possibility that, starting out—like large states everywhere —with a composite structure, it would then assume the unitary form of a state of the European type. In America, as in Switzerland and in the Netherlands, the federal structure was retained. First, as a federation of states (*Confederation*), [the Americans] fought a war of independence; but very soon after the conclusion of peace they found themselves obliged by urgent necessities of state—particularly financial—to adopt the more stable form of a federal state (*Federation*, later *Union*) (1787). The principle of separation of powers, as developed by Montesquieu, was taken over into the Constitution of the United States, but in a new and radical form which allowed the ideal of the rule of law [*Rechtsstaat*] to be realized to a degree never before attained. In the hands of a popularly elected president and a cabinet appointed by him the executive

* "Der Durchbruch des demokratischen Nationalstaates in der amerikanischen und französischen Revolution," an essay written in 1931 or 1932, but not published until after his death, in Otto Hintze, *Staat und Verfassung*, second edition, (Göttingen: Vandenhoeck & Ruprecht, 1962), pp. 503–510. Translated by Heinz Lubasz by permission of the publishers.

branch became a thoroughly independent and effectual instrument of government. Although it was obliged to work out a modus vivendi with the two houses of Congress—the representatives of the several states and of the people as a whole—it could never become dependent on the legislative branch, as happens in the parliamentary system proper. The legislative power, which was reserved to Congress, was not unlimited, as in England, but restricted by the fundamental articles of the Constitution: any law which in course of litigation was held to be unconstitutional could be declared null and void by the Supreme Court.

Among the inviolable fundamental principles of the Constitution were the rights and liberties of the individual, on which the Puritans, concerned as they were for their freedom of conscience, laid particular weight. It was in America that they were first codified, in the fundamental laws of the constitutions of the several States, and in the Federal Constitution. They were the forerunners of, and probably also the models for, the Rights of Man and the Citizen of the French Revolution. From France they in turn found their way into the constitutions of almost all modern states.

The transformation of the state by the French Revolution was indisputably influenced by what had happened in England and America. But to a considerable extent it was an independent event, and looks almost like a development intrinsic to the life of the French state.

We do not intend here to describe this development in its several phases, nor is it necessary to do so, inasmuch as it continues far into the general history of the nineteenth century, and its effects still make themselves felt today. The fundamental principles on which the modern state rests made their appearance, in theory and in practice, before the French Revolution, in England and America. But it required exceptional exertions to overcome the obstacles that stood in the way of their application to the political life of continental Europe with its distinctive historical traditions. Seen in a broad context, the significance of the French Revolution in world history lies in its having with a powerful blast cleared the way for a new era in the life of continental states. The difficulties which the new principles encountered in France—difficulties which in England and emphatically in America either did not exist, or at any rate existed to a far less degree—can be traced to three important and weighty circumstances.

In France and other continental states the feudal social structure was so deeply entrenched, and the development of the nobility's social and political privileges had reached such unsalutary heights, as to create an unbearable social tension. In America, on the other hand, no such structure existed at all; and in England it had at an early stage been transformed into a graduated class system which was permeated by a middle class spirit. The English gentry, an upper middle class which comprised members of both the aristocracy and the bourgeoisie, was able to assume the central role and the leadership in the state's modern political life. But in France the aristocracy, which was the largely idle beneficiary of the old monarchical regime, had first to be brought down to the social level of the third estate by being completely shorn of its privileges. Thereupon the free bourgeoisie, whose members enjoyed equality of status, became the foundation of the nation's new political system [Staatsordnung]. Hence the new system had a democratic cast from the outset. At the same time it came into sharp conflict with a kingship which was intimately linked with the spiritual and temporal aristocracy by historical bonds, a conflict which ended with the kingship, because of its relations with antirevolutionary forces outside France, being overthrown altogether.

The second difficulty was that government and administration in the absolutist states of the continent were in the hands of a centralized bureaucracy that was entirely authoritarian in structure. The ministers at its head did not yet form a unified cabinet with clearly delimited jurisdiction and responsibility. Rather, they were simply the agents of the not clearly articulated branches of the king's council [Ratsbehörden], in which the arbitrary will of the monarch had very wide—indeed almost unlimited—scope. The creation of modern specialized ministries with clearly delimited spheres of competence is one of the lasting achievements of the French Revolution. But in France and in the continental states which followed its example the degree of ministerial independence and the nature of ministerial responsibility fluctuated greatly with the changing temper of governments of varying composition. The French Revolution also attempted to replace the bureaucracy with more liberal forms of local government, but in vain. The bureaucratic structure proved indispensable after all: in the end Napoleon, building on the system of Commissars instituted by the National Convention, created his system of Prefects, which was widely imitated on the continent and came eventually more and more to supplant the old institutions in Prussia. At the same time, however, the continental states tried with varying degrees of success, to combine this bureaucratic system of administration with elements of English self-government. Conversely, England in the nineteenth century found itself obliged to increase the effectiveness of the old institutions of self-government by adding an extensive municipal bureaucracy.

The third and probably the greatest obstacle to the success of the new principles on the continent was the more or less pronounced mili-

tarism connected with the monarchical regime, that is, the crucial position held by the standing army and its power of command, and by
military interests altogether in the overall life of the state. This militarism resulted from the constant danger of war that existed on the
continent. By contrast, Great Britain, secure in its insularity, and the
United States, with no neighbors to rival it in strength, were able to
remain free from such militarism, in consequence of which their political life attained a quite different, a more liberal character. True, they
maintained large navies. But these instruments of naval supremacy
could not be used for the domestication of subjects, the way a standing
army can, whose garrisons strangulate a whole country. It is an historical rule already noted by Seeley,[1] that the degree of freedom within
a country is inversely proportional to the military and political pressure
exerted on its borders. The geopolitical necessity which had thus given
rise to militarism in the states of continental Europe obtained likewise
for revolutionary France, once it had plunged into war with the monarchs. What began as a war of propaganda soon became a war of conquest, because France's liberated neighbors were not willing to be paid
in worthless French *assignats*. The Terror of 1793, which resulted from
foreign invasion, brought universal military service into being. Subsequently, first in the form of conscription under Napoleon, and then in
enhanced form in Prussia, where proxies were no longer permitted,
universal military service became the very pillar of the new national
state on the continent. It established a militarism that was far more
intense and thoroughgoing than that of the old Europe had been.
Nationalistic imperialism replaced dynastic imperialism. In the World
War of 1914 these tendencies in the modern state reached their acme.
In Japan they are today [1931/2] at work reshaping the ancient Orient
as well.

   This modern state, which from the end of the seventeenth century
on spread relay-fashion across the North Atlantic area and gave the
nineteenth century its political stamp, has recently under the label of
the "liberal" state been contrasted with the "absolute" state of earlier
centuries. But such a contrast is one-sided and therefore inaccurate, even
if the words "absolute" and "liberal" are replaced with "absolutistic"
and "liberalistic" (which is perhaps more appropriate, as the former
pair designate qualities, while the latter designate tendencies). The liberal tendency of the modern state is most intimately linked with the
national. But though nationalism and liberalism go hand in hand a
good part of the way, it also frequently happens that nationalism turns
against liberalism and often repulses it completely. Nationalism is the
more powerful force of the two and, in the last resort, the decisive one.

It is important, in this connection, to bear in mind that in raising its banner in the name of such cultural entities as language, the people, and the spirit of the nation, nationalism is simply the ideological counterpart of very concrete material interests. These interests have been based on the fusion of politics with economics ever since the age of mercantilism: it is precisely from this ideology of nationalism that they have received a powerful new stimulus. In the age of mercantilism the government promoted and favored but also supervised and regulated capitalism in the interests of state power. In England in the course of the eighteenth century and then on the continent in the nineteenth, capitalism took a tremendous swing upward. It became an important factor in the new bourgeois social order which gradually freed itself from tutelage to the state and came in time to confront the state as an independent force.[2] The capitalistic entrepreneurs, who were the mainstay of the national economy, were an indispensable prop for governments travelling the new nationalistic road. This can be seen especially clearly in England soon after the Glorious Revolution of 1688. In the absolutistic states of the continent the national economy was still piling up the financial wherewithal of politics and war in a state treasury while the English government, which enjoyed the confidence of the propertied classes, could, after the establishment of the Bank of England, cover increased financial needs in critical times by means of public loans which the owners of capital willingly subscribed. Hence it could dispense altogether with the accumulating of a state treasury, something which throughout the eighteenth century, for example in Prussia, was still the main object of the state's fiscal policy. The close connection between capitalism and nationalism which manifests itself in all this characterized the modern state everywhere in the nineteenth century. So the modern state could just as well be called "capitalistic" as "liberal" or "national." However, as capitalistic tendencies freely took their course, the state, which had formerly been interested primarily in furthering the interests of capital, did in time, in some of the continental countries, begin to afford more protection to the interests of labor and so once more to circumscribe the freedom of capitalism. The endeavor to mitigate the class struggle between capital and labor and to keep it within tolerable bounds also belongs to the features of the modern state.

One may wonder, finally, whether it would not be more accurate to call the modern state "democratic" rather than "liberal." Without again entering into the much-disputed question of the relationship between the concepts "liberal" and "democratic," I simply want to note that they function on different levels. The term "liberal" applies to the use of state power in a libertarian sense, that is, one which acknowl-

edges and respects the individual constitutional rights of subjects—
which is precisely how "subjects" become "citizens" within the meaning
of the modern state. The term "democratic" applies to a constitution in
which the power of the state emanates from the people. This is not a
matter of differences in degree, or antitheses, but of different phases of
one and the same evolutionary sequence from the "authoritarian" to
the "popular" [3] state, that is, from a state in which power belongs to
its bearer in his own right to one in which it is conveyed to him by the
people. Historically, liberalism is a modification of the authoritarian
state: separation of powers and individual rights and liberties are no-
table liberal institutions. Democracy as the constitution of the "popular" [3] state may well also be liberal, and historically has generally
been so, as the examples of England, America and France show. But it
can also be authoritarian and lead to dictatorship, [4] as in Revolutionary
France after 1793 and under Napoleons I and III. In the nineteenth
century the introduction of universal suffrage became the prelude to
democratic constitutions, which are as characteristic of the modern state
as are the more or less effectual liberal institutions which exist alongside
them.

If one characterizes the modern state as "bourgeois," one must distinguish the constitutional from the sociological meaning of the word.
In a constitutional sense "bourgeois" is equivalent to "civic," that is, it
signifies the civic legal equality of all the state's subjects without respect
to status by birth or occupation—in other words, it signifies abolition of
the old feudal privileges, equality before the law. But in a sociological
sense "bourgeois" means that the propertied and educated strata of the
population in fact, if not in law, enjoy a privileged position in public
life. Where the suffrage is limited by property qualifications [Cen-
suswahlrecht], the distinction [between the propertied and the unprop-
ertied] also takes a legal form; but it assuredly exists with universal
suffrage too, thanks to the fact that landed or financial property naturally makes itself felt, and to the advantages which superior education
affords in public life. Where thoroughgoing political equality is established as between the propertied and the unpropertied, the sociological
significance of the bourgeois element in political life is reduced to a
minimum; the life of political parties is dominated by the class struggle;
the unity of the state runs the risk of being sundered by factionalism;
and the modern state thus heads towards a crisis which threatens its
existence. It should, however, be noted in this connection that in such
a situation the old and firmly established democracies prove themselves
more nearly proof against upheaval than do the untried new ones. And
one must not forget that beside this internal cause of crisis and up-

heaval there exists an external cause. It springs from the transformation of the old European state system into a new world system of states, which came into full operation in the World War of 1914. As the international community has grown larger, solidarity [within states] has decreased, but nationalistic rivalry [between states] has increased. This state of affairs too, as the postwar [i.e., post-World War I] period has shown, threatens the existence of the modern state in its old historical form.

BIBLIOGRAPHY

Krieger, L., "Nationalism and the Nation-State System: 1789–1870," in Chapters in Western Civilization, 3rd ed., vol. 2, New York, 1962, pp. 103–139.
Laski, H. J., The Rise of European Liberalism, London, 1936 (repr. New York, 1962).
Näf, W., "Der Durchbruch des Verfassungsgedankens im 18. Jahrhundert," Schweizer Beiträge zur Allgemeinen Geschichte, 11 (1953), pp. 108–120.
Namier, L. B., "Nationality and Liberty," in Avenues of History, London and New York, 1952, pp. 20–44.
Palmer, R. R., The Age of the Democratic Revolution, Vol. I, Princeton, 1959
Schieder, Th., "The State and Power Politics in the Industrial Era," in Schieder, The State and Society in Our Times, London, 1962, pp. 65–83 (tr. from German).
Shafer, Boyd C., Nationalism: Myth and Reality, New York, 1955.

NOTES †

[1] John Robert Seeley: English historian; Regius Professor of Modern History in the University of Cambridge from 1869 to 1895.

[2] On the relation of the bourgeoisie to the state in the nineteenth century see the essay by David Harris, "European Liberalism and the State," below, pp. 72–90.

[3] The German word "Volksstaat" has no precise equivalent in English, though "republic" is a fair approximation in some contexts. The admittedly awkward phrase "popular state" is used in order to convey the distinction between the state centered on its ruler and the state constituted by its population, and to avoid the gratuitous suggestion that such a state as the latter is necessarily democratic.

[4] On this point, see the essay by G. Kitson Clark, "The Modern State and Modern Society," below, pp. 90–103.

† These are Editor's notes.

# EUROPEAN LIBERALISM AND THE STATE *

## David Harris

*Bourgeois liberalism in the early nineteenth century strove to limit the power of the state, and especially to keep the state from interfering with economic activity. But by the close of the century, as Professor Harris (Stanford University) indicates, some Liberals turned to "the doctrine of the state as an engine of social betterment," while others sought "state intervention in economic enterprise for the direct benefit of the bourgeoisie."*

Europe has had an ancient tradition of dreams dreamed and deeds done in the name of human freedom. In the eighteenth century there arose in diverse parts of the continent a demand of unparalleled insistence for still more of the boons of freedom. Alas, however, for human plans; when in 1789 the opportunity came to build the new Zion with the precious stones of liberty, the builders in Paris went down in discredit and carried with them, seemingly, the repute of their great ideal. Ruined once by its mistakes, liberty in France suffered a second disaster in 1799 at the hands of a military adventurer.

A whole company of literary men exorcised the ghost of this departed horror, but with all their pages they could not write a lasting epitaph. By 1814 the people of France had become aware of the price they had paid for Corsican glory, and it was Boneparte's own creatures, his senators, who deposed him for his despotic doings and who tried to exact a sworn constitution from the aged wanderer who was then on his way to Paris as the eighteenth Louis. The new sovereign could not readily negotiate with a Napoleonic legislature on what God had already decreed, but no one saw more clearly than did this exile-weary Bourbon the impossibility of turning back the calendar to the epoch of divine right despotism. In May of 1814 he announced that he would give his people what he termed a liberal constitution and shortly thereafter he issued the charter which had its source in his royal pleasure.[1] Within

---

* David Harris, "European Liberalism in the Nineteenth Century," in *American Historical Review* 60 (1954-5), pp. 501-26. The last portion of the article (pp. 517-26) has been omitted for reasons of space. Reprinted by permission of the author and the editor.

the next six years, despite the rigors of the reaction, constitutionalism achieved a series of victories—in the Netherlands, in Poland, and in several of the German states.[2]

Louis XVIII's charter and these kindred constitutions represented the perpetuated gains of the revolutionary epoch, the level reached after the up of the excesses and the down of the reactions which had been in process since 1789. They represented, no less, the point of departure for the subsequent change, and have, therefore, a not unimportant part in the history of nineteenth-century liberalism. Indeed, these constitutions are of such significance that one perhaps may speak of the years following 1814 as the period of liberalism by princely grace.

For one reason, these instruments, with a single exception, gave guaranties of substantial individual rights. The ideal of 1789 still in 1814 embodied a living force that could not be denied. First and foremost were those two equalities without which any pretense toward modern liberty would have been a mockery—equality in the presence of the tax collector and equality before the judge and his books of law. There were, in addition, assurances that the individual would enjoy strictly regular processes at the hands of an independent judiciary, and that his property would be safe from the hand of royal caprice. Finally, the individual received a pledge that there would be no restraint on his conscience, that the exercise of his religion would be undisturbed, and that freedom of the press would be abridged only by laws to prevent abuse.

A further reason for suggesting the phrase "liberalism by princely grace" lies in the fact that there were in these constitutions two other renunciations of royal authority: henceforth no tax was to be collected and no law inscribed on the statute book without the consent of a legislative body. By such concessions there disappeared—at least on paper—those two powers which lay at the base of the absolutism of the Old Regime.

At the same time, there was another side to this newly minted royal coin. Louis XVIII was quite explicit in asserting that the plenitude of authority in France rested in the person of the king. In his proud words was a complete denial of a right belonging to the people, and with it a disquieting implication that what the king's grace had given the king's grace could take away. In substance the same theory presided over the other constitutions. Over and beyond this issue of theory was the fact of great daily significance—the predominant role which the sovereign retained for himself in his absolute veto and in his right of legislative initiative, and, too, in his periodic flaunting of self-imposed limitations.

The legislatures prescribed in these constitutions were typically bicameral. The upper house was a house of privilege in which men sat by right of noble birth, ecclesiastical office, or royal appointment. The lower house was either based on a geographic representation, as in France, or on some adaptation of the old estates system.[3] But whichever way the chamber was recruited, three devices made it certain that the deputies would bear no stain of the unhallowed procedures of 1792: first, a set of qualifications for voting which, in somewhat varying degrees, excluded the economically less fortunate; second, a scheme of indirect elections; and, finally, a still more exacting set of qualifications for the deputy. In substance these devices assured that men of maturity and property elected men of still more maturity and of still more property. As was the case in the estates assemblies of the Middle Ages, the sovereign consulted, not with his people, but with the possessors of rural and urban wealth.

At best, then, liberalism by princely grace was a meager compromise with modernity. It was, none the less, gravid with significance. The concession of personal rights and liberties revived for the Continent some of the breath of those winds of freedom which had blown so fiercely during the French Revolution. The limitation on royal taxing and legislative power had its modern as well as its medieval aspects. The restoration of assemblies, semi-estate in character though they were, at least brought several continental countries along the political road already traversed by the English.

In 1820 more advanced ideas of liberalism announced themselves from below the level of princely grace. The Spaniards, wearied with one of the most obscene governments of all Europe, restored their constitution of 1812 with its basic principle of the sovereignty of the nation, and the noise of their revolt returned sympathetic echoes from Portugal and the Italian peninsula where life was hardly better.[4] The time was not ripe, however, for inexperienced liberals to fumble with their destiny, and armed force effectively restored what was called order.[5]

The real beginning of the new chapter of liberalism's history had to wait until 1830. Its opening pages were written in France. When the crisis came in July, it was the republicans of Paris who, more than anyone else, sent the former count of Artois on his second road to exile; but in the final showdown a group of less doctrinaire deputies had greater political strength and it was they who put the imprint of their ideas on a revision of the charter. Formally, this revision was nothing more than a modest legislative retouching of the text of 1814, but the cumulative effect of the changes added up to a substantial modification of the constitutional structure of France.[6]

Meanwhile the first response from abroad had come from Brussels.

In Belgium French influences had already been inculcating their lessons of liberty and, given the signal from the July revolution, self-styled liberals and Catholics joined forces to declare their national independence and draw up a constitution.[7] So fully did this Belgian constitution of 1831 epitomize the main currents of liberal opinion in Europe that for half a century and more it enjoyed high prestige as a masterpiece of political wisdom and its provisions steadily made their way into other constitutional experiments.

In Great Britain the happy tidings from Paris created no upheaval, but they did give a new inspiration to the agitation for reform. It was an old habit for malcontents of the Continent to look across the haze of the Channel and see in England the home of liberty. In truth, the English had so far preceded the continentals that issues which preoccupied the latter after 1814 had long since been settled. Yet, despite this historical advantage, the crystallization of the estates system had produced in England an issue which was the basic issue of the Continent as well. That was, of course, a reasonable share of political power for the middle class. On this point the two liberalisms converged in time and problem. The British counterpart of the continental troubles, the great Reform Bill of 1832, averted rather than accomplished a revolution. An alliance between landed and city wealth was an old fact of English history; the new bill simply brought it up to date by effecting a more acceptable division of political power.

These political changes in France and Belgium and Britain between 1830 and 1832 charted the main direction of liberal hopes in other lands during the years that followed. Since they represented the program of a liberalism sufficiently victorious to give practical effect to its major objectives, they established the new benchmarks in the political terrain beyond the realms of princely grace.

With respect to the control of the state, there was at least a hint of a dilemma in the liberals' position. The old suspicions of the state which went back to Seneca and Augustine had found more than vindication at the hands of John Locke and his rationalist successors, and their children of the new generation were not without the family trait. On the other hand, there was a mundane consideration which also had an imposing history. Harrington had pointed it out back in the seventeenth century: that the possessors of economic power are not content until they gain political power commensurate with it. For all of the aura of dubiety about the state—indeed, on account of it—the state was a reality worth a great deal of effort to influence and to control.

None the less, the liberals of the first half of the nineteenth century did not desire to push forward to a complete mastery of the state: being moderates, they were prepared to leave old elements of privilege. Still, the share which they demanded for the middle class was materially greater than that allowed by the charters handed down from sovereign thrones.

The first victorious act of the continental liberals, following the precedent of England, was to settle their case against the undue pretentions of royal authority—without destroying monarchy. In France King Louis Philippe had to proclaim his dependence on the national will,[8] and the constitution of Belgium was most precise in its theoretical and practical curbs on kingly power.[9]

The great positive achievement of the liberalism of these years was to build up the strength of the lower legislative house. Bicameralism remained, but the place of the nobility in the body politic suffered a new reverse. In Belgium an elected bourgeois senate, in France a house of peers in which nobility had a declining role, in Britain a house of lords under notice that it must bow to the will of the nation—in such developments was eloquent proof that the liberals were attacking the custom-grounded pre-eminence of the noble estate.

The dissatisfaction with which the middle rungs of the social ladder looked upward did not prevent their turning to look downward with even less friendly eyes. These men of the middle, and their fathers before them, had once read earnest lessons about people being born and remaining free and equal in rights. But now those days were gone. The memory of revolutionary experience, the more recent evidences of proletarian unrest, the disposition of the successful to see moral failure in a humble station in life—all these considerations afforded grounds enough to deny the lesser orders of mankind a share in the great prize of political power. The upshot was that liberalism pronounced against political democracy; control of the state remained the privilege of men of property.[10]

With respect to what the state should do, a movement dedicated by tradition and by conviction to liberty had naturally a marked prejudice, if not an entirely clear principle or program. And that was, manifestly, that the state should no nothing more than the minimum required by some vaguely defined social necessity.

To keep government within the bounds of common sense, the liberals pinned their hopes to two devices. The first was a scheme to make the machinery incapable of quick or efficient action. Recalling the old tyrannies of royal despotism and the later tyrannies of the mob spirit, these twice-bitten men wished, as the abbé Sieyès said, to quench the fires of Rousseau's popular sovereignty by the waters of Montesquieu's separation of powers. The European constitutions, following the American adoption of the old principle, effected therefore a distinction between the executive, legislative, and judicial branches. In their prescriptions of bicameralism they also hoped to insure a check on hasty legislation. None the less, while an independent judiciary retained its position, very shortly the newer principle of ministerial responsibility so undermined the old that the separation of powers as a part of the credo of European liberalism was gradually pushed off into limbo.[11]

The second, and far more important, device for restraining government was, of course, the confirmation and the amplification of the bill of individual rights which the restored sovereigns had already rescued from the wreckage of the French Revolution. By its prescriptions *all* men, in their persons and in their property, were to be secured against tyranny; *all* men were to be free to think and to believe and, within limits, to write as they wished.

When one moves on into the story of the role which these early liberals assigned to the state in relation to economic enterprise, one point stands out in all clarity: the protection of property from foreign aggression, from state encroachments, from the disorders of the mob, and from the tricks of rascality. Among these last, the refusal to honor a contract was of prime and horrifying significance, since contract made the difference, so thoughtful men believed, between order and chaos.

In such unquestioned necessities there was a large and, unhappily for the liberal, an expensive role for the state—that of the self-denying night-watchman. In a positive work of facilitating economic enterprise, the stopping point of state action was not so readily established. For such things as a stable currency and the improvement of roads and harbors there was soon no serious opposition, but a fairly general liberal rejection of protective tariffs came slowly, and policy toward the new railways ranged from British private enterprise to Belgian state operation.

None the less, the prevalent theory, and increasingly the practice, left a wide latitude to the self-interest of economic man. Under its inspiration legislatures poured out a veritable stream of acts which removed qualifications from property rights,[12] extended freedom of contract, and struck ancient shackles from commerce and industry and finance. Before the middle of the century, the social consequences of industrialization were beginning to creep from England to the Continent, there also to raise grim questions of policy; but the rank and file of the liberals, genuinely humanitarian though they were, found it hard to reconcile themselves to state regulation. Inescapably there had to be a great deal of confusion when Europe faced problems hitherto undreamed of, and, quite apart from a powerful economic theory, there could only have been much doubt as to the ability of state agencies, given their notoriously bad history, to do an effective social service.

The practical applications of this ideal of liberty, however, betrayed an inner contradiction, an inherent conflict of purposes. The constitutional and legislative enactments bestowed rights on all men without distinction of birth or fortune. Likewise the principles of the inviolability of private property, liberty of individual enterprise, and freedom of contract vouchsafed blessings to all men equally.

But, as these doctrines worked out in daily practice, they created disparities in wealth and position which boded ill for any morally rooted concept of freedom. The high regard for property rested on the old conviction that property was essential for the full achievement of the human personality. Something was wrong, therefore—as Thomas Jefferson saw [13]—when many men had no property. Something was wrong, too, for the prospects of human personality when freedom sent the penniless factory worker to negotiate single-handed a contract with an owner, or the landless peasant to deal with a great proprietor. These pregnant years of the first half of the century were demonstrating that seemingly inescapable paradox of man's finite destiny which decrees that a liberty which is not within hailing distance of equality is not really a human liberty. It is, rather, a citadel of privilege, something alien to the birthright of all men as envisaged in Jefferson's Declaration of Independence and in the French proclamation of the Rights of Man.

When political privilege was added to the economic, the citadel was complete.

The citadel, however, rested on precarious foundations. There was hardly any man so libertarian that he was prepared to deny a paramount claim of society. In the realm of economic enterprise and, too, in the realms of intellectual and spiritual enterprise, the ends of society could be achieved in one of two ways. The most direct was by means of social controls. The liberals rejected this alternative in favor of a wide latitude of individual freedom. But, caught in their commitment to social primacy, they could do so only on one logical condition: that, by some alchemy of the nature of things, there presided over free individual activities a benignant and harmonizing force which served the high claims of social justice. In a very literal sense, therefore, the liberalism of the first half of the century was nailing its case for freedom, for the full realization of the potentialities of the individual personality, to the future fortunes of capitalism.

It was difficult to provide a systematic justification for the position taken by these early liberals. An overt appeal to the heady doctrines of

Natural Law was hardly feasible. Only a few were aware of how David Hume had used his scalpel,[14] and Jeremy Bentham his brass knuckles,[15] on that ancient mode of thought, but many were well aware, since the French Revolution, that Natural Law contained a far more dangerous set of axioms than the purposes of liberalism needed.

Nor was there much greater security in the utilitarianism preached by the genial sage of Ford Abbey. Bentham's ponderous writings also went too far. They were good for criticizing an outworn order, and they gave the liberals much needed help with their economic problems, but, when pushed by logic, Benthamism produced not liberals but radicals, radicals who were disposed at times to turn their syllogisms against the liberal order as well as against the old. Bentham himself demonstrated the radical potentialities of his method; he allowed his reasoning to lead him into democracy and republicanism and, no less to the consternation of the liberals, he impatiently laid down the thesis that there was no assignable boundary to the sovereign power of the state.[16]

Liberalism, therefore, had to feed on a different kind of meat. In England it was not bad form to go in for fairly systematic thinking about economics, but in politics it seemed safer to respect what was popularly considered the national distrust of an abstract proposition. In France the liberals were content—were, rather, compelled—to go through the motions of philosophizing while dodging the basic problems of political philosophy.[17]

But however deficient this early liberalism was in a sound philosophic foundation, it was not wanting in uncritically embraced assumptions. To name some of them is to see the trick played upon itself by a professedly antimetaphysical generation: the belief in an abstract individual who stood in antithesis to the state, the sanctification of private property to the point that no liberal, or even Benthamite, was willing to subject it to the test of social utility, and, finally, the assurance that the selfish activities of atomistic individuals would, under that invisible hand celebrated by Adam Smith, add up to a maximum social benefaction. These foundation assumptions, one need hardly point out, were simply old Natural Law concepts carried over bag and baggage into the new century. For the time being, however, a philosophic inadequacy lay obscured behind material and political success.

In 1848 there burst over Europe a new revolutionary fury. For a fleeting moment many a liberal glimpsed a day of new triumphs, but only for a fleeting moment. That frenzied year was compounded of a variety of suddenly unleashed forces and they served notice, at times in brutal language, that the future did not necessarily belong to liberalism. Yet, for all the power of upsurging competitors, and for all the triumphs of the old order, liberalism defied the current epitaphs and went on to the period of its greatest victories. If liberalism after 1848 was living on borrowed time, it made good use of the loan. Liberalism in the first half of the century had been more a state of mind, a set of impulses, than the doctrine of a single political party. Gradually parties took shape which claimed to act as the special custodians of the credo and their services to the cause were great. Theirs, however, were by no means the only services rendered. The whole work of the great day of liberalism was not a monopoly product of party spirit, but the effect rather of a pervasive flow of conviction.

After 1848, as after 1814, the triumphs of reaction did not entail a complete turning back of the clock. In Italy the *statuto* of Piedmont-Sardinia remained in force; [18] in Prussia a king who had recently advaned strong religious reasons for his despotism felt obliged to refashion a revolutionary document into a constitution emanating from his sovereign grace,[19] and his successor in 1867 accepted as a matter of course a written instrument for the North German Confederation, a document which, with slight modification, became the constitution of the German empire in 1871.[20] In the Habsburg dominions new attempts at personal rule broke down and the *Ausgleich* of 1867 was a victory for constitutionalism as well as for Hungarian national feeling.[21] This successful pressure went on until finally, before 1914, there was no state in Europe without some formalized procedures of calculable government. These gains, of course, had their uneven qualities when measured against the liberal ideal; at the same time, the continuing direction of European political development was seemingly beyond all doubt.

A signal feature of this heyday of liberalism was a great expansion of individual liberties. Not all police interference was confined, by any means, to Russia, but generally in Europe one individual freedom after another gained formal recognition and became more solidly embedded in social practice.

Among the freedoms most cherished by liberalism was that of religion. This zeal for an unrestrained right to worship as the individual saw fit, plus the inherently secular cast of liberal thought, precipitated serious conflicts with ecclesiastical authorities in the second half of the century. A perhaps inescapable series of clashes with Catholicism was made all the more certain by the determination of Pope Pius IX to strengthen the ultramontane forces within his spiritual dominion. Liberalism's response was a further reduction of church influence, state appropriation of ancient ecclesiastical functions, and denunciations of concordats by which earlier popes had hoped to tighten the bond between crown and altar. In Great Britain the tendency of legislation was in the same direction: disestablishment in Ireland, termination of the Anglican monopoly at Oxford and Cambridge, and progressive emancipation from various forms of religious disability.

As for economic liberty, the steady march of freedom in international trade from Huskisson's enactments, through the repeal of the Corn Laws and the Cobden-Chevalier treaty, on to imperial Germany's first economic legislation, is an oft-told tale. Equally representative of the strong current of liberalism was the victory of freedom in domestic enterprise. Nowhere was this conquest of a free economy more sweeping than in Germany. On top of administrative reforms and the rigorous application of the principles of the *Rechtsstaat*,[22] German capitalism received independence so readily and so generously that its practitioners —unlike their predecessors in England and in France—never felt a driving necessity to win a political victory as a means of achieving economic freedom.

These great accomplishments were all aspects of the question of what the state should and should not do. In these same years after the middle of the century that other basic political question, the control of the state, was equally hammered on the anvil of controversy.

The formalized structure of government as inherited from the first half of the century continued to be a compromise between king, nobles, and the new version of the old third estate. Without launching a direct attack on outward forms, liberalism none the less tended to undermine that equilibrium of forces. Over Europe as a whole liberalism continued to have no doctrinal objection to monarchy. So exceptional was the latest French experiment after 1873 that Mr. H. A. L. Fisher on the eve of 1914 was led to his ill-fortuned surmise that there was no future in Europe for republicanism.[23] Kings, however, were no longer the real issue in the problem of executive authority; the real issue was the adoption of the British device of ministerial responsibility. Where the liberals were sufficiently powerful, they secured it; where they were not, they agitated for it, and in this preoccupation the question of monarchy steadily shriveled to an irrelevancy.

With respect to the nobility, its place also was subject to a continued erosion. In England a great acceleration of the ancient process of elevation to the peerage—so deftly satirized by the wag who spoke of the house of beers—tore away much of the old substance. The final blow, within the framework of bicameralism, came in 1911 when the lords lost their position as a fully co-ordinate legislative power. On the Continent the course of formal institutional growth was different, but the end result was even more drastic for the heirs of feudal privilege.

Membership in upper houses became more and more a matter either of
election or of appointment, and there were fewer and fewer men who
could claim a seat as a right of birth.

While liberalism was chipping away at the privileges embodied in
the old compromise, its own system of privilege was suffering attacks
from two different directions. When the reactionaries of the Bourbon
restoration in France proposed the enfranchisement of the lower classes
as a means of swamping the bourgeois liberals [24] they introduced an
idea which was not easily to lose its attraction. In England an alliance
of the upper and lower social strata to squeeze the middle was a part
of Disraeli's political philosophizings, and on it he acted in pushing
through his electoral reform bill of 1867.[25] In that same year Bismarck,
moved by a variety of considerations, gave the North German Confederation a lower chamber elected by direct universal manhood suffrage.[26] In Belgium, the Catholic party, confident of the support of
the peasants, voted extensions of the suffrage over the opposition of
many of the liberal leaders.[27]

On the other side of the liberal position, the pressure toward democracy became ever greater, championed as it was by the growing power
of radicals and socialists. The dilemma for the liberals was increased
by the fact that in times of need—for example in Paris during the crisis
of the July Revolution and in Britain during the Reform Bill and
Corn Law agitations—they themselves had not been above playing
with the democratic fire. It was one thing, however, for the liberals
to use the masses, to turn them on and off like a spigot; it was quite
another to put the ballot into their hands. In addition to simple social
prejudice, practical observations showed some ominous clouds on the
horizon. There was danger that the bishops would command the vote
of the faithful for their own illiberal purposes, and there was an even
more threatening danger that a propertyless majority would lay reckless
hand on the rights of property.

Pressure and persuasion, however, were not wholly to be defied, and
gradually, hesitatingly liberalism began to move in the direction of
political democracy. Yet it could not carry with it the whole body of
its adherents. The conversion of Gladstone and the eventual splits of the
liberal party in Britain are not unrepresentative of the whole experience of Europe.[28]

A new generation of writers rose up to put their pens at the service
of the liberal cause, but the most striking efforts toward a philosophic
validation were those of two Englishmen, John Stuart Mill and
Herbert Spencer. Mill in his tract *On Liberty* made, most assuredly,
one of the world's great pleas for human freedom, yet his attempts

to refurbish Benthamite utilitarianism left his cause lost in philosophic confusion. For all of his sympathetic open-mindedness, Mill could not go beyond the old assumption that there was a fundamental antagonism between the individual and the state. Herbert Spencer tried to lodge the same proposition in the ineluctable laws of science, but the more he elaborated his system the more he turned out to be a Procrustes who hacked in vain on the intellectual child of his own procreation. It was soon apparent that science was to be no more successful in finding one voice for the discussion of politics than religion had been.

Despite this continued poverty of theory, liberalism in the second half of the century accomplished a multitudinous work. Yet the high period of achievement lasted but a brief moment. Already in 1872 Disraeli likened the liberal government bench at Westminster to a range of exhausted volcanoes.[29] One may discount the hyperbole of a political novelist in opposition, but there was percipience in his analogy. The great Gladstone ministry came to a weary end in 1874 and could not repeat its triumphs in 1880. In 1879 the recently victorious liberal republicans in France came under Clemenceau's schismatic criticisms for excessive compromise. Equally in 1879 the national liberals in Germany were losing out and their colleagues in Austria, tarred like certain liberals in other countries by the crash of 1873, were falling into disrepute. Sterility and confusion were spreading over liberal Italy and comparable symptoms of malady showed themselves elsewhere. The old liberal ideas seemed to be losing their force and the liberal parties were breaking into discordant factions.

The difficulties were of two kinds: crises within liberalism itself, and external blows from both the left and the right.

One of the great internal crises of later nineteenth-century liberalism has already been suggested: the debate on political democracy. The second was over the vexing question of what to do next. So much had been done within the old framework that the movement showed signs of reflecting John Bright's outlook, when, in 1873, he said that the great causes to which he had devoted his public life had been brought to fruition.[30] A revival of energy required a new liberal principle, and a new liberal principle depended on a new analysis of the relation between individual liberty and the state, that problem on which Mill and Spencer had produced nothing new.

The crucial decision had eventually to be made on whether something should be done by the state about the social consequences of industrialization, the old question first raised by nonliberal humanitarians earlier in the century. Some liberals had found in the iron law of wages an argument against intervention; some had been torn in mind and spirit over the issue; but the dominant voice of the movement had happily assured the anxious and the outraged that economic freedom would find the answer. The march of the years, however, did not deal gently with these responses. The logical plausibilities of the iron law of wages persuaded no one to reconcile himself to a marginal existence, and, worse still, the spread of free industry, for all of its miracles, showed no signs of binding the wounds of humanity. The meagerness of the life of the lower orders was revealing all too clearly that the old combination of certain rights for all men and special rights for certain men was not, after all, a harmonious and defensible synthesis. If liberalism was to maintain its concern for the universality of its principles, if it was to rise above the charge of being simply a pig philosophy, it was going to have to follow the nonliberals in a critical assessment of the laissez-faire state.

Both in England and in France there was noteworthy thought which helped to clarify and to solve the problem of liberalism. Within its own arsenal there was a weapon that could be put to a new use, and that was Benthamite utility. Stripped of Bentham's own cumbersome rationalizations, the principle raised the simple but searching demand that every institution and every practice should be weighed in terms of a calculable social benefit. William Stanley Jevons invoked it in an important book published in 1882. Jevons proposed to go forward empirically with social questions, assessing the good and the bad of each suggestion as it arose without tenaciously holding onto the old presuppositions against state intervention.[31] About the same time, Thomas Hill Green approached the same set of problems from the point of view of an emerging school of British idealism. Green lodged the right and the necessity of positive state activity in its assistance to the moral self-realization of the individual.[32]

In France a wide variety of students gave their attention to this question. Out of their discussions came the doctrine of *solidarité* which, like that of Green, put its emphasis on the inherent dignity and worth of the individual human being. To serve the high purpose of moral individuality, these French thinkers were prepared to place restrictions on, without abolishing as a matter of dogmatic principle, the rights of private property.[33]

In so far as it rallied to such considerations, liberalism made a new affirmation of its concern for all men. After Gladstone was gone, the British liberal party became converted to the doctrine of the state as an engine of social betterment, and these same ideas were gaining ground on the Continent when the war came in 1914.[34] This reshaping of liberal thought, however, was not easily accomplished. The conception of a positive role of the state won out only at the expense of more divisions within the ranks of liberalism, as in the case of the move toward political democracy. The social group which, a generation and more earlier, had shown a high degree of cohesiveness, was beginning to break up.

This propensity for dissension appeared at the same time in another complex issue of state intervention. Disillusionment with the happy confidence of early liberalism was by no means limited to an acknowledgment of the poor fortunes of the proletariat. Time revealed, and especially the time after 1873, that all was not well with the fortunes of the middle possessing class.

In a period, accordingly, when the state loomed larger and larger as the ark of salvation, it was inescapable that uneasy entrepreneurs should also see in this erstwhile Moloch the instrument of their own redemption. Earlier, when Europe had lived under that regime of state intervention so inaccurately called mercantilism, the "sneaking arts" of the self-regarding pressure group had put an uncountable array of laws on the statute books. In the hard times of the 1870's and later, the growing practice of turning to the state offered an opportunity which industrialists and landowners could ill afford to overlook.

The whole story of Europe's abandonment of international free trade and its reversal of colonial policy cannot be told simply as the machinations of capitalists who had lost their nerve. At the same time, the work of the Central Union of German Manufacturers and comparable societies elsewhere leaves no doubt but that, in no small measure, the return to protection and imperialism was state intervention in economic enterprise for the direct benefit of the bourgeoisie.

The rising of these issues meant further splits and defections within the ranks of the liberal parties. In spite of the continued dedication of many liberals to the "sacred principle" of free trade, in spite of hesitations about imperial adventures, liberalism was perforce to some degree driven away from its older outlook, that outlook which had in it the vision of a peaceful world joined together by the bonds of unfettered trade.

While these internal crises were racking liberalism, the movement was suffering from a costly competition. In earlier times, the ancestral set of liberal ideas had engaged in what had been essentially a straight two-sided contest. When, however, the liberals began to search out their position after the French Revolution, they found that they no longer stood face to face with one antagonist; they were, rather, caught between two opponents, one to the left and one to the right. By the fourth quarter of the century, liberalism was beginning to feel keenly the disadvantageous consequences of its middle ground.

## BIBLIOGRAPHY

Hawgood, J. A., "Liberalism and Constitutional Developments," in *New Cambridge Modern History*, vol. 10, Cambridge, 1960, pp. 185–212.

Näf, W., "Staatsverfassungen und Staatstypen, 1830/31," in *Schweizer Beiträge zur Allgemeinen Geschichte*, 3 (1945), 179–204.

Ruggiero, G. de, *History of European Liberalism*, London, 1927 (repr. Boston, 1959).

Sabine, G. H., "The Historical Position of Liberalism," in *American Scholar*, 10 (1940), pp. 49–58.

Schieder, Th., "The Crisis of Bourgeois Liberalism," in Schieder, *The State and Society in Our Times*, London, 1962, pp. 39–64.

## NOTES

[1] The essential documents are given in France, Conseil d'Etat, *Collection complète des lois, décrets, ordonnances, règlemens, avis du conseil d'état . . . par J. B. Duvergier*, XIX, *passim*. Hereafter crited as Duvergier.

[2] The constitutions under reference may be found in Great Britain, Foreign Office, *British and Foreign State Papers*, as follows: (1) The Netherlands, III, 16–43; (2) Poland, XIX, 971–85; (3) Bavaria, V, 1055–76; (4) Baden, V, 161–70; (5) Württemberg, VI, 102–30; (6) Hesse-Darmstadt, VII, 386–99. Article XIII of the Constitution of the German Confederation of 1815 prescribed that each state would have an "estates constitution" (*landesständische Verfassung*) (*ibid.*, II, 128). Among the princes of German states who issued fundamental laws more in harmony with the estates concept than did the rulers of the above cited states were those of Saxe-Weimar-Eisenach, *ibid.*, III,. 842–71; Schwartzburg-Rudolstadt, III, 747–48; Schaumburg-Lippe, III, 749–51; Waldeck, III, 751–63; Hanover, VI, 1130–33. The king of Prussia anticipated the decision of the Confederation to the extent of announcing on May 25, 1815, his intention of preparing a constitutional act and of establishing a representative assembly (*ibid.*, II, 1057–60), but he could take himself no further along the constitutional road than the organization of a council of state in 1817. The text of the instituting decree may be found in *ibid.*, IV, 791–99.

[3] In the Netherlands members of the lower house were named by the provincial assemblies. In Poland a majority was chosen by the noble dietines and a minority by the communes. In Bavaria five separate categories were represented, in Württemberg six, and in Hesse-Darmstadt three.

[4] For the text of the constitution signed at Cadiz in 1812 see *State Papers*, VII, 237–79. The Portuguese cortes on March 9, 1821, decreed the bases of a new constitution (*ibid.*, VIII, 973–77), and the definitive text was promulgated on September 23, 1822 (*ibid.*, IX, 921–59).

⁵ For a convenient collection of the principal documents relative to the conferences of Troppau and Laybach of 1820–21 and the suppression of the constitutional movement in Naples see *State Papers*, VIII, 1129–1206. For the conference of Verona and the decision to suppress the Spanish difficulties see *ibid.*, X, 909–36. On June 25, 1823, the king of Portugal issued a proclamation annulling the constitution and appointing a junta to prepare a new constitutional draft (*ibid.*, XI, 852–53).

⁶ Duvergier, XXX, 93–103; 110–14; *State Papers*, XVII, 1009–13, 1013–18.

⁷ For the text of the Belgian constitution as voted by the national congress on February 7, 1831, see *State Papers*, XVIII, 1052–65.

⁸ Because of the delicacy of the crisis in July and August, 1830, it was essential to proceed tactfully with the revision of the charter. The declaration of the chamber, adhered to by the peers, disposed of the theoretical issue of sovereignty in these words: "Selon le voeu et dans l'intérêt du peuple français, le préambule de la Charte constitutionnelle est supprimé, comme blessant la dignité nationale, en paraissant *octroyer* aux Français des droits qui leur appartiennent essentiellement" (Duvergier, XXX, 94–95). In his act of August 9 Louis Philippe said, "J'accepte, sans restrictions ni réserve, les clauses et engagemens que renferme cette déclaration et le titre du Roi des Français qu'elle me confère, et je suis prêt à en jurer l'observation" (*ibid.*, XXX, 104).

⁹ Article 3 of the Declaration of the Rights of Man and Citizen in 1789 states, "Le principe de toute souveraineté réside essentiellement dans la nation." The Spanish constitution of 1812 took the sentence in this form: "La soberanía reside esencialmente en la nación" (Title I, chap. 1) and the Portuguese document of 1822 repeated it (Title II, art. xxvi). The declaration of the French chamber in 1830, as indicated in the preceding note, repeated the adverb *essentiellement*. The Belgian constitution-makers dropped the adverb as an unwarranted equivocation: "All power emanate from the nation . . ." (Title III, art. xxv).

¹⁰ For the text of the French election law, April 19, 1831, see Duvergier, XXXI, 177–219. This law raised the number of voters from about 94,000 to about 188,000. In Belgium the more generous suffrage qualifications were determined variably from province to province. The Reform Bill of 1832 increased the number of British voters from about half a million to slightly more than 800,000.

¹¹ Benjamin Constant (Henri Benjamin Constant de Rebecque) offered an ingenious argument in support of a system of five powers (*Cours de politique constitutionnelle* [Paris, 1818–20], I, *passim*). François Pierre Guillaume Guizot, *Histoire des origines du gouvernement représentatif et des institutions politiques de l'Europe* (Paris, 1855), translated as *History of the Origin of Representative Government in Europe* (London, 1861): "Il faut qu'il y ait plusieurs pouvoirs égaux et indispensables l'un à l'autre, dans l'exercise de la souveraineté de fait, pour qu'aucun d'eux ne soit conduit à s'arroger la souveraineté de droit" (I, 122). Charles Edward Merriam,

Jr., *History of the Theory of Sovereignty since Rousseau* (New York, 1900), chap. v. Jeremy Bentham launched an attack on the doctrine of separation of powers in *Fragment on Government* (1776) reprinted in *Works* . . . ed. Sir John Bowring (Edinburgh, 1838–43), I, part 1.

[12] For a discussion of the increased freedom of property in England see Albert V. Dicey, *Law and Public Opinion in England during the Nineteenth Century* (London, 1905), pp. 200 ff.

[13] Jefferson to the Rev. James Madison, Fontainebleau, Oct. 28, 1785, Julian P. Boyd, ed., *The Papers of Thomas Jefferson* (Princeton, 1950–), VIII, 682.

[14] In *Treatise of Human Nature,* first published in 1739–40.

[15] In *Anarchical Fallacies: A Critical Examination of the Declaration of Rights,* written about 1791, in *Works,* II, part 2, pp. 489–534.

[16] For the development of Bentham's radicalism see Elie Halévy, *The Growth of Philosophic Radicalism* (New York, 1928), pp. 254–65, 415, and *passim;* Leslie Stephen, *The English Utilitarians* (New York and London, 1900), I, chap. vi.

[17] For further discussion see Roger Soltau, *French Political Thought in the Nineteenth Century* (New Haven, 1931), introduction, chaps. i. iii; Guido de Ruggiero, *The History of European Liberalism* (London, 1927), pp. 158–73. Henry Michel, *L'idée de l'état* (Paris, 1896), p. 291; "Les Doctrinaires sont pauvres de doctrine, ou, si l'on aime mieux, leur doctrine consiste tout entière à expliquer, à justifier certains états de fait."

[18] An English translation by S. M. Lindsay and Leo S. Rowe may be found in *Annals of the American Academy of Political and Social Science,* supplement to Vol. V (1894–95).

[19] For the text temporarily accepted by the king of Prussia on December 5, 1848, see *State Papers,* XXXVII, 1378–90, and for the text of January 31, 1850, *ibid.,* XXXIX, 1025–39. A translation and commentary on the latter document by James Harvey Robinson may be found in *Annals of the American Academy of Political and Social Science,* supplement to Vol. V.

[20] For the constitution of the North German Confederation, 1867, see *State Papers,* LVII, 296–313, and for that of the empire promulgated in 1871, *ibid.,* LXI, 58–76.

[21] For the text of the "December Constitution" of Austria, December 22, 1867, see Edmund Bernatzik, *Die österreichischen Verfassungsgesetze mit Erläuterungen* (2d ed., Vienna, 1911), pp. 390–453.

[22] For an introductory and illuminating discussion of German theories of the relation between the state and the individual from Kant through Jellinek see Ruggiero, part I, chap. iii.

[23] H. A. L. Fisher, *The Republican Tradition in Europe* (New York and London, 1911), chap. xiii.

[24] In 1815 the leading *ultras* of the chambers, at odds with the government of Louis XVIII and critical of the charter, asked for a wider suffrage. Villèle explained as follows: "From the beginning of the world . . . the

middle class, envied by the lower and an enemy of the upper, has constituted the revolutionary party in all states. If you wish to have the upper
class in your assemblies, have it chosen by the auxiliaries which it has in
the lower class, go as far down as you can and thus annul the middle class
which alone is the one you have to fear" (S. Charléty, *La Restauration
[1815–1830]* [Paris, 1921], p. 98).

[25] For brief summaries of Disraeli's political thought see Crane Brinton,
*English Political Thought in the Nineteenth Century* (Cambridge, Mass.,
1949), pp. 130–48, and Robert H. Murray, *Studies in the English Social
and Political Thinkers of the Nineteenth Century* (Cambridge, 1929), I,
chap. VI.

[26] For a number of years Bismarck had been moving toward the decision of 1867. On the one hand he was increasingly aware of the advantage
for Prussia in German politics of an advanced position on suffrage. On the
other, he had had more than occasion, since his advent to ministerial power
in 1862, to regret the kind of majority which the three-class electoral system
had sent to the Prussian Landtag. An astute student of Napoleon III,
Bismarck well knew how the latter-day Bonaparte had capitalized universal
suffrage for his own purposes. From 1862 to his death in 1864 the
socialist Ferdinand Lassalle had pushed the Prussian minister-president
toward broad electoral reform.

[27] Frans van Kalken, *La Belgique contemporaine (1780–1930): histoire
d'une évolution politique* (Paris, 1930), p. 124; Jules Garsou, *Frère-Orban*
(Brussels, 1945), pp. 87–105.

[28] On May 11, 1864, Gladstone startled a routine House of Commons
debate by saying, "I venture to say that every man who is not presumably
incapacitated by some consideration of personal unfitness or of political danger
is morally entitled to come within the pale of the Constitution" (*Hansard's
Parliamentary Debates*, Commons, 3d Ser., CLXXV, 324). John Morley,
*The Life of William Ewart Gladstone* (London, 1905), I, 759–65. One of
his most irreconcilable colleagues in the liberal party was Robert Lowe, later
Lord Sherbrooke. In the spring of 1866, during a new debate on suffrage
extension, Lowe made a notorious attack on the idea of working-class suffrage, in which he said, among other things, "If you want venality, if you
want ignorance, if you want drunkenness, and facility for being intimidated;
or if, on the other hand, you want impulsive, unreflecting, and violent people, where do you look for them in the constituencies? Do you go to the top
or to the bottom? . . ." (*ibid.*, 3d Ser., CLXXXII, 147–48). In France there
appeared in the writings of Charles Renouvier and Emile Littré a hope to
have a bourgeois pre-eminence within the framework of universal manhood
suffrage. For an introductory exposition and a useful bibliography see John
A. Scott, *Republican Ideas and the Liberal Tradition in France, 1870–1914*
(New York, 1951), pp. 47–115. Emile Faguet belonged to the liberals who
refused to make their peace with democracy. See his *Le libéralisme* (Paris,
1902), *Culte de l'incompétence* (Paris, 1910; English ed., London, 1911),
and *L'horreur des responsabilités* (Paris, 1911; English ed., New York, 1914).

[29] William Flavelle Monypenny and George Earle Buckle, *The Life of Benjamin Disraeli Earl of Beaconsfield* (New York, 1929), II, 530–31.

[30] George Macaulay Trevelyan, *The Life of John Bright* (Boston, 1913), pp. 411–15.

[31] William Stanley Jevons, *The State in Relation to Labour* (3d ed., London, 1894).

[32] Richard L. Nettleship, ed., *Works of Thomas Hill Green* (London, 1894–1900). "Lectures on the Principles of Political Obligation" may be found in Vol. II, and "Liberal Legislation and Freedom of Contract" in Vol. III. David G. Ritchie, *The Principles of State Interference* (2d ed., London, 1896), chap. IV; John MacCunn, *Six Radical Thinkers* (London, 1907), chap. VI.

[33] Charles Gide and Charles Rist, *History of Economic Doctrines* (New York, n.d.), pp. 587–607; Francis W. Coker, *Recent Political Thought* (New York, 1934), pp. 410–15; Scott, pp. 157–86; Michel, *L'idée de l'état*, pp. 581–622.

[34] The principle of the state as an agency of social reform must be distinguished from the proposition that the economically privileged classes should attempt through legislative benefactions to assuage the dissatisfactions of the less fortunate. This latter doctrine was articulated in a rough frankness when Joseph Chamberlain in 1884 and 1885 began to speak of the "ransom" which property would have to pay for its security. Charles W. Boyd, ed., *Mr. Chamberlain's Speeches* (London, 1914), I, 130–39; J. L. Garvin, *The Life of Joseph Chamberlain* (London, 1932–51), I, 541–43. A comparable thought appeared in France in the writings of Emile Littré, who wished to undermine the revolutionary nature of the proletariat by a policy of "social conciliation" (Scott, pp. 100–5).

# THE MODERN STATE AND MODERN SOCIETY *

*G. Kitson Clark*

*Industrialization, the rapid growth of population, the rise of metropolitan slums, and the stresses and strains of capitalism have created problems which do not solve themselves, and which private initiative has not*

* G. Kitson Clark, "The Modern State and Modern Society: Historic Tendencies and Future Probabilities," reproduced from the *Proceedings of the Royal Institution of Great Britain* 37 (1959), pp. 551–65, by permission of the Editor and G. Kitson Clark.

*been up to solving. Mr. Kitson Clark (Cambridge University, England)*
*sketches the historical background of the "demand for greater social jus-*
*tice" and shows that, in response to this demand, the modern state in*
*the twentieth century has been carrying through a real or pretended*
*"social revolution," under the auspices of either the Welfare State or*
*socialism.*

The object of this discourse is to try to see whether by looking back
to the relevant past it is possible to discover what general tendencies
and principles have come to control the organized communities in which
we live, and therefore *may*, obviously that word must be italicised, direct
the development of those communities in the future.

In order to conduct such an enquiry at all accurately it is necessary
to define two words: *State* and *modern*. The definition of the first word
is relatively easy. The *State* is the *Community* organized for the purposes of *government*. It is to be differentiated from the *community*
which may be held to mean the whole body of people, nation, towns-
folk or whatever they may be, who live together as a group, united by
common ties and common feelings no doubt, but not under consideration as an organized entity; it is to be differentiated from the *government*, which I hold to mean the administration and constitutional
machinery which controls and organizes the community. These differenti-
ations are important because in order that a government may effectively
organize a community there must be some common theory, some focus
of common intention or at least some common habit of mind which
makes men and women work together and obey the law. Therefore to
understand a *State* you must not only understand the system of government but the ideas behind it also.

The other word to be defined, the word *modern*, presents greater
difficulties. Clearly it means what is pertinent to the present and to the
relevant past—that portion of the past whose overriding tendencies and
dominant principles survive into the present and are likely to be extended into the foreseeable future. But how are we to determine what
part of the past is relevant? What meaning are we to put on the word
"modern" in terms of actual years, or events, or phenomena?

One way of settling this problem might be to choose a date and to
say that everything after that is "modern." This method is much used
by the writers of University ordinances to define at what date papers
on modern history are to start, or who are to be qualified for a Professor-
ship or Lectureship in modern history. It is a way of proceeding which
is more satisfactory for the purposes of administration than those of
scholarship but if a date is to be chosen for the beginning of the modern

world I would suggest 1917. In 1917 the first great war had gone on for three years. The old Europe which had engendered so horrible a catastrophe was morally bankrupt, even in Great Britain the idealism with which the war had been started had begun to fade into cynical disbelief. The chief contestants had been bled white, and were on the margin of exhaustion; in fact one of them, Tsarist Russia, had stumbled and fallen. This was an end and a beginning, for from the agony of Russia emerged a new kind of State, of great significance for the future.

The State which came into existence after the Russian revolution was a communist state, but what is probably more significant, it was a *totalitarian* state. Such a state is normally the result of a revolution, the programme of which it presents in its institutions and intention, and which has wiped off the slate the values of the pre-revolutionary world. The State is totalitarian because it claims to sum up in its own purposes all the values it accepts or considers to be valid, and for this reason its demands on its subjects are total, there are no values beyond, or irrelevant to, the purposes of the State to which they can appeal. If its subjects serve the purposes of the state they are fulfilling the only legitimate object of their lives; if they are deemed to have betrayed those purposes or if they cease to be particularly useful to them, or if their elimination would serve those purposes better than their survival, they are expendable.

In the next thirty years other total States came into existence, some in sympathy with, some in antipathy to, Communist Russia. The two best known, Fascist Italy and Nazi Germany, were antagonistic to communism, but their polity bore a strong resemblance to that of Russia. In each there was the rule of the dictator endorsed by the rule of a single party. In each all the institutions of the state and of the community —the machinery of justice, the organization of education, the press, the Trade Unions—were subordinated to the ideas of the party. More than this, the regime in each of these countries derived in part from the sufferings of the war of 1914–18 and the defeat or failure of those who had ruled the country before 1914. The Russian revolution was the result of exhaustion in war and the utter failure of the Tsardom. Italy was nominally one of the victors of the war, but she found the fruits of victory extremely disappointing and after the war she went through a period of serious social disorder, with which the singularly uninspiring Parliamentary regime she had inherited from before 1914 dealt very ineffectively. Germany had been defeated in 1918, the defeat was followed by the inflation and then after a recovery came the financial collapse of the early thirties and the advent of Hitler.

In fact these new states were the result of frustration, a frustration which cancelled and discredited what had gone before. But one force which was not cancelled by what had happened between 1914–1917 or afterwards, was nationalism. Whatever the appearances Russian nationalism was not cancelled by the Russian revolution, and it came to the rescue of the Russian Communist State in striking fashion in the hour of its great peril in 1941 and 1942, and it need not be said that nationalism was in the forefront of the Italian and German revolutions. This is significant because nationalism is still one of the most potent forces of the modern world, moving and stirring in all quarters of the globe. The demands which it makes on those subject to it are often total. It is an irrational force not a coherent political philosophy, but it sometimes puts itself forward as a self sufficient creed, as it sometimes uses a variety of ideologies—communism, fascism, democracy—as cover under which to work. Its nature is not I think well understood, and that I am afraid is the fault of my profession, for we historians have not subjected the various national movements to sufficiently searching objective historical analysis.

On the other side of the scene in the modern world are the *liberal democracies*—the Scandinavian States, Holland and Belgium, France, Great Britain and the British Dominions, the United States, India and a number of other States. A liberal State has certain characteristics. In a liberal State the subject is protected by what is known as the *rule of law*. He is not supposed to live his life at discretion—that is to live or to die, to enjoy liberty or to suffer imprisonment according to the momentary convenience of the government. If he is to be restrained or punished it must be according to the provisions of a law known beforehand, judged by someone who is not the servant of the government and after a trial the procedure of which has some relationship to what are known as "the principles of natural justice". The law must protect him, as far as possible, in the enjoyment of certain rights, such as the freedom to worship as he pleases and freedom of discussion and association, etc. It must secure that his opinion on the government to which he is subject is taken at regular intervals at elections which are protected by expedients which have been proved to be necessary to secure free elections, as for instance voting by a truly secret ballot, the right for more than one candidate to compete without hazard to himself and adequate laws against bribery and intimidation.

Such are the characteristics of the Liberal State, and they are based on one common principle. The Liberal State accepts the belief that human beings as human beings can serve values which transcend the possible objects of the State, and that apart from those objects they possess rights with which the State did not endow them but which it must respect if it can. Most Liberal States have however something else in common. Most of them came into existence before 1914, they were the victors in the war of 1914–18 or the neutrals that escaped it, except for modern Western Germany and Italy which have been forcibly reconverted to Liberalism as a result of the war of 1939–45. Liberal democracy is in fact an old creed based on principles which were accepted before the end of the nineteenth century, some of them long before the end of the nineteenth century. This indeed shows the danger of choosing a precise date to designate the beginning of what you are to call modern; such an attempt leads to the belief that what existed before your chosen date is not likely to have contemporary relevance, or is automatically less likely to be influential or to survive than anything that came into existence after that date. There is a great deal of historical evidence to suggest that this simple view of things is normally a vulgar error. But it is true that anything which is to survive in the world as it exists now must accommodate itself to the conditions which prevail today. Those conditions are in many ways the same for all states, totalitarian or liberal, and therefore all existing civilized states, totalitarian or liberal, share in part the same characteristics, use some of the same principles and to some extent pursue the same ends.

Some of these common characteristics have a long history behind them, as for instance has the fact that all modern States are *Sovereign States* or aspire to be *Sovereign States*. A Sovereign State is autonomous, it is the sole judge of its own actions, no appeal lies to anyone against it. The sovereignty of Sovereign States is most often considered in the international sphere, in connection with a State's autonomy in its relations with other Sovereign States; but it is important to remember that it exists in the domestic sphere also. In a Sovereign State the subject has no legal right against the State at all, the power of the State is absolute. This is palpably true of the total State, but it is true of the liberal State also. It is true of Great Britain. In Great Britain the subject has important rights against the executive, he can sue the policeman, the soldier, the borough official, Her Majesty's government itself, if he believes they have infringed his rights. But he has no rights against the law. In England a rule which is an acknowledged part of the English Common Law or the result of a statute duly passed by King, Lords and Commons, may seem to an Englishman to be absurd, unjust and generally intolerable, but he must obey it or take the consequences. There is a moral restriction on the actions which a liberal State may take against its subjects and it is very valuable, but there can be no legal restriction on those actions.

This doctrine of sovereignty has a long history behind it, in its modern form it probably stretches back to the claims made by the French monarchy of the thirteenth century when confronting the claims of the papacy of Boniface VIII, or to the nature of the Italian States of the fourteenth and fifteenth centuries; and the history of European States in the sixteenth and seventeenth centuries suggests that internal sovereignty is necessary for a successful common life, that organized life becomes impossible if the law can be successfully challenged in the name of the vagaries of the individual conscience or of indefeasible ancient right or privilege. There is no reason to believe that that necessity has disappeared, but so absolute a rule requires a general justification which all will accept, if it is to be effective. If law is to be Sovereign then there must be some generally accepted principle which makes all ordinary men obey the law.

There have been many such principles in the past. Laws have been obeyed because they were an inheritance from the ancients, because they were believed to embody the will of God or to represent the law of nature. But to men of our generation, who do not accept prescription as a source of right, are not likely to agree on what is the will of God or whether there is a God to have a will, and do not use the conception of nature as it was used in the old theory, none of these answers are likely to be satisfactory. There is indeed only one answer which is nowadays likely to be accepted generally enough to do what is necessary, and this suggests a second characteristic common to all contemporary governments. They are all *Democracies,* the moral sanction behind the law in all of them is that the law is conceived to be the will of the people.

This is of course true of the liberal democracies, but it is also true of the total dictatorships. They are often called nowadays "people's democracies," their courts are normally called "people's courts," and their dictatorships are considered to be the most effective way in which the will of the people can be made to prevail. Indeed, on occasion this may be true, the actions of a dictator may, for a period, represent the desires of a people more truly and embody its will more effectively than the results of the compromises and manoeuvres of a Parliamentary democracy. Since a dictatorship is irresponsible there is no assurance that those actions will continue to embody the people's will, but whether they do so in reality or only in pretence, or even if that will is more correctly interpreted by properly organized Parliamentary elections, the theory of democracy remains morally unsatisfactory and not a little dangerous.

After all the will of the people is more or less of a fiction. At best, it is the will of the majority, and it is difficult to see what gives a majority a moral licence to override the essential rights of a minority. This is most obviously objectionable in the case of a relatively large racial group which is in a more or less permanent minority, but the rights of any minority however small raise some difficult questions. Unfortunately democracies have not been very ready to entertain any questions about the extent of their power or the comprehensive character of their moral rights. In fact, probably since Rousseau, certainly since the Jacobins in the first French Revolution, the leaders of democracy have shown a tendency towards totalitarianism, a tendency which can be studied in the important work on the *Origins of Totalitarian Democracy* by my friend Professor Talmon of the University of Jerusalem. This tendency is made much stronger when a new democracy is the instrument of irrational emergent nationalism, as it normally is.

Yet it is difficult to avoid accepting democracy as the working political theory of a state, simply because no other theory nowadays seems tolerably morally satisfactory or likely to win sufficient general acceptance. Where it has been established for some time it may be hoped that a certain tolerance has been developed and it might be held that in mature States its dangers could be disregarded if it were not for the fact that the general ethical assumptions of modern politics, and the normal physical conditions of modern life also tended to press the Modern State towards an ever-increasing assumption of power.

For instance in order to satisfy the public conscience every modern state is carrying through, or pretending to carry through, a social revolution. Since as long ago as the eighteenth century men have been anxious to correct the inherited inequalities of society and enable all to live a fuller life in a juster community. At first, men were apt to believe that this could be secured if the classes who had seemed to batten on the old prescriptive inequalities of society—the kings, the nobles and the priests—were removed, but it soon began to seem clear that a more positive social revolution with a more drastic redistribution of property was necessary. The shadow of this appeared in the course of the first French Revolution, but the demand had become much more clear by the revolution of 1848. This demand for greater social justice, or, in less theoretical terms, the desire to correct positive injustices or causes of suffering, has had certain important practical results for the institutions of the modern state which can perhaps be best studied in the very practical history of nineteenth century Britain.

What often happened in Britain has been well described recently in an article on "The Nineteenth Century Revolution in Government" by Dr. Oliver MacDonagh in the *Historical Journal* (Vol. 1 (1958), 52–67). Britain was in the early nineteenth century, from about 1820, a country with a lively, observant and very free-spoken press, it was beginning to have a rather uneasy social conscience and there prevailed conditions in various parts of the country which were always bad for large sections of the community, and could very easily become very dreadful indeed. As a result there were in fact a succession of scandals which were exposed by the press or by active reformers, and which attracted the attention of the public and of Parliament. Legislation was then normally passed to put things right, which, since it was framed by men who were ignorant of what had to be done and had no machinery to enforce it, was almost always completely ineffective. At the next attempt therefore Parliament would not only pass legislation to remedy the evil, but also appoint officials—commissioners, inspectors and the like—to bring the act into effect, and to report on the way it worked. The turning point in this process is probably 1833. At the beginning of that year certain ex-naval officers were appointed to inspect ships in the various ports to see that the acts passed to protect the unfortunate, and much exploited, emigrants were put into force, and later in the year factory inspectors were appointed to watch over the acts passed to protect the factory children.

As soon as this was done two things happened. In order that these officials should do what was wanted of them they had to be granted considerable discretionary powers, both to frame regulations and to put them into effect—the powers granted to the early factory inspectors were extraordinarily wide, and the officials began to develop their own specialized knowledge of the conditions which they were handling, which was necessarily the starting point for new legislation—the most important parts of the Factory Act of 1844 derive from the recommendations of the factory inspectors. From such beginnings as these there has been built up the tremendous machinery of state which now confronts us with its vast power to make regulations to control our lives, and its mass of expert knowledge from which new policy derives. That development was necessary if we wished to improve conditions which desperately needed to be improved. Men and women could not be liberated from disease, ignorance or exploitation in any other way; but it is to be remembered that men and women liberated by the strong arm of the State are not liberated in every sense of the term. Power is power, it makes people do what they do not want to do and prevents them from doing what they want to do, even if on the whole it is exercised for their good, or what other people conceive to be their good. More than this, all this work costs money, which must be raised from taxes and rates. This can of course be justified, it is a way in which, to some small extent, wealth can be redistributed, those who are better off paying for what is necessary for those who have been less lucky. But the State is not like Robin Hood taking from the rich and giving to the poor, it takes from the rich certainly but it keeps what it takes. It will no doubt spend it on what is good for the poor, but that is rather different from giving it to the poor to spend for themselves. To an increasing extent there is a concentration of wealth in the hands of the State, and a concentration of wealth must inevitably mean a concentration of power.

This concentration of power was not only demanded by the social morality we all have come to accept, it was rendered unavoidable by the necessities of the world in which we all have come to live. From some time in the eighteenth century there had been an enormous increase in the population of these islands. The figures before the first census in 1801 are very uncertain, but by 1801 the figures for England and Wales were still under 9 million, by 1901 they were 32,527,843. No one knows what started off this increase, it was not the industrial revolution, for it took place in Ireland where there was no industrial revolution. But it may be said that if these vastly increased numbers were to be maintained with an improved standard of life, and, in the end, a generally improved standard was going to be provided in England and Wales and Scotland in the second half of the nineteenth century, then the new methods of production were necessary. Indeed they were probably necessary if life was to be maintained at all. In Southern Ireland there was no effective industrial development yet by 1845 the population had risen to (about) 8,250,000. By the census of 1851 it had fallen to 6,552,385 for between the late summer of 1845 and the end of 1847 there had been a failure of the potatoes and it is calculated that Ireland had lost about two million people, roughly one million by emigration and one million by death as the result. Such indeed was the possible fate of a population which depended for its life not on industry or on developments in technology but mainly on one article of primary produce.

But if the new methods of production were necessary to sustain the life of the new great population and ultimately to improve its standards some other things were also necessary to make life possible in the new conditions. The new methods of production drew people into large towns. In Great Britain the *addition* to the numbers of people living in towns of over 20,000 inhabitants was 1,100,000 between 1821 and 1831, 1,270,000 between 1831 and 1841, and 1,800,000 between 1841 and 1851. The new industries drew them into the towns, and the new towns slew them. They could not do otherwise, they had few or no sewers except to carry away flood water and men did not really know how to make a sewer which could be relied upon to carry away anything else. They had not enough water, and men did not know how to procure enough water. There was no adequate housing, the new millions had to be stowed into the nooks and crannies of old decaying property, or hastily built slums. There were no adequate authorities, local or central, to control the situation. The results were too horrible to be described here, and the death rates in the towns rose to—in some cases—very terrible figures.

The battle against these conditions took place roughly between 1842 and 1875. The leaders in the assault were doctors like Kay and Southwood Smith and administrators like Sir Edwin Chadwick. As far as the knowledge of that day went they were experts. They did not know what carried infection, for Pasteur and Koch did their work too late to be of use, but they got to know what conditions and what areas were likely to breed infection and how to try to get rid of those conditions. They were helped by some engineers, by Parliament on occasion and very greatly by enlightened local authorities; and after a good deal of of trouble and the final personal defeat of Chadwick in 1854 it became clear between 1870 and 1880 that the battle was being won. The death rates of certain important killing diseases—typhus, typhoid and scarlet fever—began to drop off just before or just after 1870, there was no serious cholera epidemic after 1866, and the general death rate started to go down. Before 1870 it was normally about 22 per thousand live persons, in Liverpool and Manchester much worse than that, and it starts downwards after 1870 sinking to 18.1 per thousand in the years 1891–1900 and in 1900–1910 to 15.2. Moreover what has been held to be most significant for the general wellbeing of the population, the death rate from tuberculosis sank from 3.6 per thousand in 1851–55 to 1.9 per thousand in 1896.

Now three things are significant about this battle. Victory in it was necessary if a reasonable life was to be lived in these islands, for it must be remembered that disease not only kills, it mauls—it leaves misery, degradation and impoverishment among the living. The campaign was necessarily based on expert knowledge. At first it gained initial impetus from public agitation, but what had to be done could only be understood by those doctors and administrators who were gaining an expert knowledge of the task in hand. These were not matters on which the views of the general public could have any relevance. In the early 1850's there was a lively public debate on whether the best drainage for a town was by means of the relatively small egg-shaped pot sewer or by large brick culverts which a man could enter and clean. It was a futile debate because the matter could only be decided not by voting but by experiment carried out and judged by those actually engaged on the work. Indeed as time went on the problem was less and less submitted to public debate and became more and more a matter for expert consideration, so much so that it has often escaped the attention of historians and many people by no means realize how important was the work done in what was probably the most critical period—that between 1854 and 1866, or what was the full stature of the hero of it, Dr. John Simon. . . .

The work was essential, it was expert, it was largely done behind the scenes often by careful persuasion; but in the end compulsion had to be used. Dr. John Simon said of the great public health act of 1866 that by it—"The grammar of common legislation acquired the novel virtue of the imperative mood." If that virtue was novel in sanitary matters in 1866, its novelty must have worn off pretty quickly after the string of Acts which were passed on health and housing between 1866 and 1875; nor did the law on many other matters than health and housing remain unfamiliar with that mood. In fact the lesson is this. Leaving social reform aside, the terms on which life was offered in the mid-nineteenth century made careful regulation imposed by the categorical imperative of the expert a matter of necessity unless the most intolerable conditions were to ensue, and what was to be offered to many was not life but death.

In the twentieth century, life has become more complicated, more artificial, and the population larger, and from 1906 onwards a more drastic policy of social reform has been put in hand. On top of this there have been two wars in which national survival could only be secured by fusing the whole community into a single sword in the hand of the government, and as a result during each of them there developed in Britain a closer administrative control over the life of the country than has been realized at any time in the history of most other States and certainly not in Britain before, the lessons of which the executive has never forgotten. Since the last war, a difficult economic situation has developed which has entailed close supervision by government experts of the control of such things as large-scale capital investment and the use of foreign currencies, whatever party is in power. As a result, Great Britain has developed the incredibly formidable machinery of government which controls so much of our life by the ever-increasing network of regulations, against which such bitter complaint is made.

Yet Britain is a Liberal Democracy, and indeed other Liberal Democracies are going along the same road at a greater or less speed. In fact, since it seems that every Modern State must develop this tremendous supervisory power, since every Modern State claims the absolute autonomy of Sovereignty, since every Modern State must invoke the all-justifying theory of Democracy it may be asked whether there is now any real difference between the Liberal and the Total States, beyond a certain difference of degree in practice.

The answer is, of course, that there is a very great difference, that that difference of degree in practice relates to the points which are most critical for human freedom and represents a great difference in theory about ultimate values. But that does not mean that modern conditions do not menace the values of the Liberal States. They do, and at two points.

There is danger to come from the irrational force of nationalism. Nationalism seems to me to be the wild beast in the human arena. We cannot argue it out of existence or suppress it and ought not to try to do so but, as I have said, I believe we could do more than we have done to study it objectively, neither adulating it and automatically excusing its excesses, nor condemning it, but trying to understand it.

Nationalism presents probably its most serious problems to emergent or thwarted nationalities, the problems presented by the influence of the expert and the technologist over the lives of men are universal. Without their help and direction, life as we now live it would be impossible. The industrial revolution was partly based on advances in technology, and since it started, improvements in technology have given the inhabitants of Europe and North America an immensely improved standard of life which they would not willingly surrender and no doubt higher standards are on the way, but to achieve them we must allow those who are to plan the technological advance pretty free discretion. As I have tried to show, without expert control over the conditions of life so many millions could not contrive to live together at all in such close proximity as we do in Britain. We must depend on the directions of the expert, how far then can we control him? In very many matters popular control must be a myth. It is unlikely that large sections of the general public will have enough general understanding of the difficult problems of advanced economics, administration, technology, etc., involved in his work to enable it to have coherent opinions on how that work should be conducted, and if it had such opinions the results of a vote would not seem to be a very satisfactory way of settling a difficult technical question. These essential questions must to a large extent be outside politics, but they may affect very decisively the things which politics are supposed to be about and the demands of the expert and the technologist may touch very closely on matters which seem to affect the essential values of society.

If this is so perhaps we ought to think out rather carefully what we mean by democracy. It is not, however, what the expert may ask which is the real point of danger, it is what he may give. He normally gives it to someone else to do with it not what he would desire them to do, but what that other person thinks fit, for it is never the expert as an expert who provides the government. And what the expert has to give to government nowadays may be illimitable power. This fact is usually nowadays expressed in terms of the gift to governments by one section of scientists of the hydrogen bomb, but it is important to realize that modern techniques have not only added immeasurably to the power which a modern government can use externally against its enemies— which may be checked by the thought of what its enemies might use in reprisal, but that these techniques have also added to what it can use internally against its subjects to balance which there is likely to be no counterpoise.

As Budapest showed in 1956 the utmost heroism is of little avail against modern weapons used without interference from abroad and without compunction. Probably by the terms of his life a factory worker in a modern town is easier to tyrannize over than a peasant in a prim- itive countryside. Nor is the power which has been given over men's bodies the only thing to be considered; there is also the new power which has been given over their minds—and may be given in fuller measure in the future. The modern techniques of advertising and publicity have been developed into the science of propaganda, and the development first of the wireless and now of television has endowed governments with uniquely effective instruments for putting over propa- ganda to a whole nation. Fortunately, a certain element of human stupidity, a failure to realize that one-sided monotony breeds in the end boredom and disbelief, seems so far to have limited the effectiveness of these weapons. But even so government propagandists have in vari- ous countries in the last forty years made more people believe what was demonstrably false than would have seemed remotely possible in the days of Huxley and J. S. Mill when men believed in, not only the *sanctity*, but the *power*, of the appeal to reason and the ascertainable fact. However, there are more sinister probabilities. One of the most striking examples of the way in which the results of a perfectly objec- tive scientific enquiry can be used for terrible purposes can be perhaps seen in the way Pavlov's experiments on dogs have been apparently used to perfect the technique of what is called "brain washing," and as more is learnt *about* the mind and brain, as psychologists and surgeons learn for therapeutic purposes to do more *to* the mind and brain, so also in all probability are techniques developed for those who wish to fasten the domination of one mind upon another.

This is an age of many nightmares, but there is no reason why they should turn into realities. I am no believer in historical determinism: I believe that man's future is in his own hands. As I said earlier on, the fact that the values of the Liberal States derive from a world before 1917 does not mean that they will not survive, in full force, after 1959. There is, however, I believe, one condition for their survival. Something of the nature and history of those values and of the principles upon which they have been based must continue to be understood by the ordinary educated man. If that is crowded out of his education and consciousness then those values will be crowded out of a world, which will very speedily forget them as if they had never been.

### BIBLIOGRAPHY

Barker, Ernest, *The Development of Public Services in Western Europe, 1660–1930,* London, 1944.

Bruce, M., *The Coming of the Welfare State,* London, 1961.

Carr, E. H., *The New Society,* London, 1951 (repr. Boston, 1957).

Childs, M., *Sweden: The Middle Way,* New Haven, Conn., 1936.

Fay, S. B., "Bismarck's Welfare State," in *Current History,* 18 (1950), pp. 1–7.

Mowat, C. L., "The Approach of the Welfare State in Great Britain," in *American Historical Review,* 58 (1952), pp. 55–63.

Robson, W. A., *The Welfare State,* London, 1957.

Toumanov, V. A., " 'Le Welfare State': est-il un myth ou une réalité," in *Journal of World History,* 7 (1962), 212–224.

# TOTALITARIANISM IN THE MODERN WORLD *

## George F. Kennan

*In his long and distinguished career in the Foreign Service of the United States, Mr. Kennan has seen service both in Nazi Germany and in Communist Russia. It is perhaps partly owing to this circumstance that he is free from the very common but very grave error of regarding Communism and Fascism (or Nazism, which is a particularly virulent form of Fascism) as virtually identical forms of total domina-*

---

* Reprinted by permission of the publishers from *Totalitarianism,* edited by Carl J. Friedrich. Cambridge, Mass.: Harvard University Press, Copyright, 1954, by the President and Fellows of Harvard College.

*tion. The talk of which the following is the principal part was given in 1953, i.e., prior to the program of liberalization undertaken by Khrushchev. This should be borne in mind in reading what Mr. Kennan has to say concerning the possibilities of liberalization in a totalitarian regime.*

When I begin to think of totalitarianism as a general phenomenon, the first thing that assails me is, as usual, the problem of definition. That there is such a thing, I have no doubt; but how does one delimit the term in such a way as to make it a useful one for purposes of group discussion? We have all noted totalitarian elements and tendencies in every human society, including sometimes our own; but to me the only places where these tendencies have really flowered and revealed their true nature seem to have been Germany and the Soviet Union. Some people would argue about this, I know. They would suggest that other countries as well should be included under this heading. Let us leave this argument aside for the moment, and agree that there are at least no *better* examples than Germany and Russia, and that these might then be permitted to serve as a basis for discussion.

But even here I run at once into difficulties; for I see that the Russian and German phenomenon were highly disparate things, in nature as in origin; and I am moved to wonder whether there is any generic phenomenon that we can identify and describe from actual experience as totalitarianism. Is there really some identity of essence as between Russian Communism and German National Socialism? Or is it simply that two countries have both had certain national experiences in our time and that those experiences have simply had points in common, perhaps accidentally?

When I try to picture totalitarianism to myself as a general phenomenon, what comes into my mind most prominently is neither the Soviet picture nor the Nazi picture as I have known them in the flesh, but rather the fictional and symbolic images created by such people as Orwell or Kafka or Koestler or the early Soviet satirists. The purest expression of the phenomenon, in other words, seems to me to have been rendered not in its physical reality but in its power as a dream, or a nightmare. Not that it lacks the physical reality, or that this reality is lacking in power; but it is precisely in the way it appears to people, in the impact it has on the subconscious, in the state of mind it creates in its victims, that totalitarianism reveals most deeply its meaning and its nature. Here, then, we seem to have a phenomenon of which it can be said that it is both a reality and a bad dream, but that its deepest reality lies strangely enough in its manifestation as a dream, and it is by this manifestation that it can best be known and judged and discussed. This conclusion, involving as it does a most profound contradiction, is already an unsettling and baffling one to the simple bureaucratic mind; and I can only back off from it and pass it on to the philosophers with my best wishes and regards.

Leaving aside, then, the question of definitions, and turning to the nature of whatever it is we conceive to be totalitarianism: there are a number of things that occur to me about it and seem to me to be significant. Whether they constitute an adequate list of its important attributes, I strongly doubt. I cannot say that they build up to any reliable conclusions. They remind me of the observation (I forget the origin) that "we have chaos, but not enough to make a world." Anyway, let me list some of them for you and tell you what I think they may mean.

First of all, I have been greatly impressed with the primary importance, in the totalitarian picture, of modern police weapons and their use. I am thinking here not merely of arms and munitions; I am also thinking of such things as modern means of transportation and communication. Whenever, today, a group of men obtains a monopolistic control over these things and exercises that control with sufficient ruthlessness and with suitable techniques, for the purpose of perpetuating its own power, and so long as that group retains its internal unity and does not suffer violent interference from outside, popular revolt is simply impossible. In this fact there seems to me to lie the fundamental reality of modern totalitarianism; and I would point out that this is a reality derived from the progress of modern technology.

Whether totalitarianism was conceivable apart from modern technology, I do not know. I have heard it said by well informed people that all the essential features of Soviet Communism could be observed in certain ancient oriental despotisms. I cannot be a good judge of this, for I know nothing about oriental history. I would be inclined to doubt that this could be wholly true, precisely because of the importance of the technological component in the totalitarian system as we know it today. In any case, so far as the West is concerned, totalitarianism does seem to have been something made possible only by the technological developments of the past century and a half, which have operated to enhance enormously the potential scope and intensity of absolute power.

Noting that, my mind turns next to the question of popular support —that is, the relation of totalitarian power to the feelings of people. Here I notice that there have been great differences between the Nazi and Soviet phenomena. In Germany, Nazi rule certainly enjoyed at most times a fairly high degree of mass support—although whether this would have continued much longer, had Nazi power not been destroyed when it was, seems to me to be doubtful. In the Soviet Union, Communism was introduced by a small minority and has been maintained the same way. The Soviet regime enjoyed the passive tolerance of the masses at the time of the seizure of power, largely because of the lack of promising alternatives, and in consequence of certain demagogic concessions it made to popular feeling at the moment; but it has never been the product or the object of mass enthusiasm. No majority was ever necessary to Bolshevism. People in this country have a seemingly incurable tendency to overrate the propaganda successes of Bolshevism. I am not aware that anywhere in the world, unless you insist on including China in this picture, has Soviet Communism ever won over a majority or commanded mass support; in no case, certainly, has propaganda been the main source of the establishment or maintenance of its power; in no place has it ever come into power except by force of arms—by pressure, that is, exerted either by the direct application or by the threat of armed force.

This being the case, a great deal that has been written about totalitarianism on the basis of experience with National Socialism has turned out to be not fully applicable to Soviet Communism. This is true, it seems to me, of a good part of the teaching concerning the importance of the cultivation of mass delusions, and the creation of scapegoat elements on which to focus mass emotion. These things always have been present in totalitarianism in one degree or another; they have been really important, on occasions, to the seizure of power; but they are important to the maintenance of power only if a serious attempt be made to maintain real mass enthusiasm. The Soviet rulers make no such attempt. They do, of course, in a rather half-hearted and routine way, employ both devices: the myth and the scapegoat. Now, for example, two decades after the final and official liquidation of the "remnants of capitalism" in Soviet society, lacking any other plausible scapegoat element, the Soviet rulers are not averse to gleaning such meager profit as can be gleaned from the exploitation of the endemic, and not really very powerful, anti-Semitism in certain sections of the Soviet population. But they do this only when it coincides with considerations of foreign policy. And as a domestic measure, they do not exaggerate its importance. Their rule actually rests not on the cultivation of illusions but on a bitter reality: which is the existence of a monopoly of physical force and a readiness to employ that monopoly quite ruthlessly in the interests of the perpetuation of the power of the ruling group. The mystique and semi-religious appeal are important for the promotion of Soviet purposes in areas where Soviet power is not yet dominant; where it already reigns supreme, they become subsidiary elements.

It is true that the effective application of Soviet police power involves the use of certain devices peculiar, as far as I know, to modern totalitarianism, namely, the maintenance of a system of artificial tensions within society (as a substitute for the natural ones, which might be dangerous to the system) and the employment of coercion on a vast scale for what might be called prophylactic purposes (that is, the concentration-camp system) in place of, or in addition to, its use on a small scale for the punishment of actual offenses, as in bourgeois democracy. It involves, in other words, as you all know, the punishment of people primarily for the crimes they have not committed, rather than for those they have—the punishment of those who might rebel, rather than those who *do*. It even involves, precisely for this reason, a species of intimacy and collaboration with the real criminal element in society, since the latter are necessary to provide certain of the essential features of the early purgatory: the trusties and the yegg-men, the tormentors of the political prisoners and exiles. These—not, as many people suppose, the degree of terror—are the features of modern totalitarianism, incidentally, that seem to distinguish it from most of the traditional forms of despotism.

But none of these things have anything to do with mass support, really. They are only addenda to the system of police intimidation. This being so, popular emotional support must be viewed as something which may or may not be a feature of totalitarianism, but is certainly not essential to it. What is essential is only the seizure, organization, and ruthless exercise of power. For the seizure of power, a certain degree of mass bewilderment and passivity are required—in other words, certain negative rather than positive states of the mass mind. Once power has been seized, even these states of mind are not vitally important.

Now modern police weapons are of course only one of the essential components of the totalitarian situation. Another is the presence of a body of men—namely, the natural bureaucrats and enthusiasts of a police regime—ready to use those weapons for the purpose indicated. I would like to say that I think such people are always present in any human society, to some degree or another. They are not a product of the political movement itself. They are something that is always there and needs only to be activated. They represent a mutation of the human species. I do not need to describe these people to you, nor is it pleasant to do so. They merge with the born criminal element, to which I have already referred. They are the brutal, aggressive, unsuccessful natures, deficient in moral courage, in self-confidence, in self-respect, in the ability to compete on any even terms. They are the ghouls of human society. In the sunlight of normalcy you do not see them. But let society be overtaken by the darkness of some special weakness, which leaves it helpless and vulnerable, and they are suddenly there, slinking out of the shadows, ready to take over, ready to flog, to intimidate, to torture, to do all those things in the company of armed men, and preferably against unarmed ones, that help to give them the illusion of success and security, that dispel for the moment the nightmare of inadequacy by which they are haunted.

Such people, I reiterate, are always there in every human society. They are all around us. They are the people of whom Dostoyevsky's totalitarian, Verkhovensky, said in *The Possessed*: they "are ours, though they do not know it." They are the Judases of whom any political society would be justified in saying: "Behold, the hand of him that betrayeth me is with me on the table." But in most instances, they become real dangers only when the weakness of society is already present.

It is these reflections that bring me to think of modern totalitarianism as a sort of a strait jacket which can conceivably be clamped on to any great modern society if and when circumstances so dispose. To use another word picture: it is a condition made possible by modern police weapons, a state into which any great national entity *can* relapse, if it doesn't watch its step. Whether it might be considered a natural state for peoples of other climes and eras, I do not know. But for Western man, taught as he has been to look for hope and solace in the dignity of the human spirit, it is surely a pathological, abnormal state— a sick state, devoid of hope, characterized by the deepest sort of agony and misery and depression.

It is a state, furthermore, from which there is no recovery, I fear, by the patient's own effort. Only three things can, as far as I can see, operate to bring it to an end. One is successful military intervention by external power. A second is forgetfulness and lack of due vigilance and zeal on the part of the totalitarian rulers themselves. The last is the disruption of the unity of the ruling group. But to the last development, totalitarianism surely has a certain congenital vulnerability in its dependence on the individual dictator and in its lack of any reliable institutional framework for the transfer of power from one individual to another. The lack of such a framework is precisely one of the things that distinguishes it from dynastic absolutism, as indeed also from bourgeois democracy. Just in these days it is useful for us to bear in mind, I think, that the ultimate test of totalitarianism lies not in its ability to surmount peaceably any single crisis of succession but rather in its ability to survive what is bound to be a long series of such crises, each attended by great nervousness and fear and secret intrigue, and sure to